The Routes of English

2

by Simon Elmes

B B C RADIO 4

Published by BBC Education Production
201 Wood Lane,
London W12 7TS

Commissioning Editor: Angie Mason
Editor: Anne Barnes
Design: Graphics International
Picture research: Caroline Jackson
Production Manager: Helen Whitaker
CD Replication & Studs: The Data Business
Printing: Geoff Neal Litho Ltd

FOREWORD BY MELVYN BRAGG

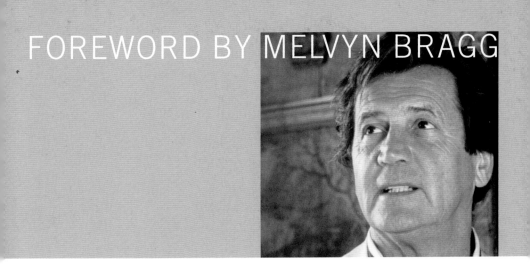

When you start broadcasting you think that the audience is listening to you. The longer you stay in the trade you realise that much of the fun and interest is that you are listening to them. It is an exhilarating and painless way to absorb a map of Britain.

Judging by the letters and other responses to *The Routes of English* we live in a country widely inhabited by people in love with the language they speak. As a democrat it is deeply satisfying to learn that this affection crosses all backgrounds and classes. As a writer I was often put to shame by the care and detail in the letters which came in. And, as a citizen of this country, I felt that I was surfing on great waves of affection and respect for a language which, however much we bend it and twist it and savage it and elaborate it and intellectualise it, constantly refreshes itself and binds us together like nothing else.

We called in experts, we called on fanatical amateurs and we knocked on the door of Everyman and woman. In this second series we concentrated on themes - new words, word play, swearing, class etc. - and the contributors provided just as much variety and vigour as before.

INTRODUCTION BY SIMON ELMES

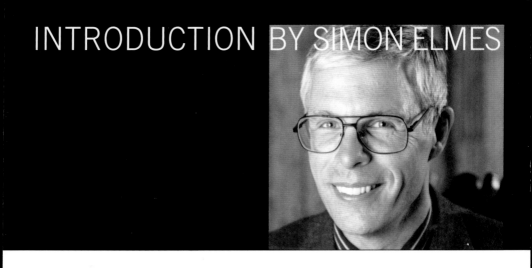

Following the routes of English across a thousand years of history is a journey that takes us through the dark Anglo-Saxon forest and then the golden plenty of Renaissance English. It takes us past eighteenth century formality to the wild articulate playground of language today.

In the first book, we traced the path of the language from six geographical starting points. In this second book, we have taken five basic thematic targets - linguistic dartboards as it were, each with a big idea as the bullseye. From each of these ideas the social and historical consequences ripple out. We start with a birth - the birth of new words. There is perhaps no subject more fitting in a book about language, at the start of the first century of a new millennium, than the idea of newness. It is one of the most mesmerising, and yet utterly simple, qualities of language: the power to create from nothing. We meet people like Simon Luke, for whom the business of making up new names for products is his business. Cut-throat, tough and often with nothing to show for it at the end, this inventor role is a powerful one in language, especially when a new product name, like *Prozac, Kodak, escalator* or *sellotape*, is patented and finds itself, shortly afterwards, in the dictionary.

If the power to invent impresses, how about the power to make someone laugh?

Language at play is the subject of our second chapter, embracing the funny business of using words to make people laugh. Language play is so diverse, as you can discover between these pages, involving as it does the mantra-like burblings of the infant, the acrostical mania of the Victorian enthusiast intent on composing poems containing only one vowel, and the alliterative power of the Anglo-Saxon in the heat of battle. You have been warned!

What is clearly required is a better class of language. The complex conundrum of 'speaking proper' is opened up in chapter three. Taking the British obsession with matters of class as the bullseye, the rings of 'correct' and 'common', 'refined' and 'vulgar' speech spread out like circles. Why was Keats condemned for his 'Cockney' rhymes when Wordsworth got away with Cumbrian sounds that were unknown to the fashionable London intelligentsia? Blame Thomas Sheridan and 'Elocution' Walker. Who they? Turn to chapter three.

Chapter four looks at unspeakably bad English. The whole bloody business of swearing, oaths and bad language comes in for expert scrutiny, and not without a few revelations, such as why we say 'rabbit' and 'donkey' rather than use the words our ancestors would have favoured.

The final destination in this journey along the routes of English is a favourite of mine -

and of the many correspondents who write to us at the BBC: namely the fraught affair of 'Thou shalt not'. Should we or should we not try to stop the mighty roar of the English language in its tracks and prescribe the form it should take? Should we say that one usage is 'good' English and another 'bad'? Should we take every opportunity to 'put right' what are seen as solecisms? Or are those pedants who have wished to freeze the great river of English to make it perfect merely linguistic Canutes?

How order was created, and then overwhelmed, by the flood of words pouring over the weir into the twenty-first century, is the story of the spoken language's final chapter, and the last stop along the Routes of English. It's quite a journey!

contents

1

COINING IT

A version of AA Milne's story about Winnie the Pooh, translated into Esperanto. Esperanto was developed over a hundred years ago as a 'second language for all', which people could learn easily and which would avoid the political problems of national languages when used for international communication. There are millions of people around the world who use it all the time.

Have you ever sat down, maybe when you were a child, and decided that you'd had enough of speaking English and that you were going to invent a new language? It is far more common a pastime than you would imagine. Sometimes a new language has to be created to give people a common understanding of a particular subject or range of ideas such as a new development in the field of engineering. At other times it is the need for a secret language, a way of creating a barrier to communication rather than widening it, which gives rise to a new language. Families often assemble a vocabulary of their own which can be used to exclude outsiders. Children in school or people in prison often develop a vocabulary and pattern of expression in order to baffle those in authority over them. Sometimes, of course, new languages are set up in order to maintain class barriers or to define and protect an elite.

People researching languages in Britain have found a vast cottage industry of language-coining going on right across the country. Some of these made-up languages have been far-fetched and exotic: one was entitled *Lalpen* after the inventor's preferred breakfast cereal. Some are full of random arrangements of 'phonemes' (sounds) that could form potential words in English; others have more logic to them, complete with origins which can be easily traced and clear grammatical structures. Throughout the world, changing circumstances bring a need for a new mode of expression and sometimes this amounts to a whole new language. This is not a new development. At the end of the 19th century in Warsaw, Professor Lazarus Zamenhof dreamed of a world in which everyone would speak an international language. By selecting elements from a range of different languages he came up with *Esperanto,* a system inspired by the hope that communication barriers could be broken down, bringing peace and understanding to the world, if there was a world language

WINNIE-LA-PU

AN ESPERANTO VERSION OF
A. A. MILNE'S *WINNIE-THE-POOH*

Translated by Ivy Kellerman Reed
and Ralph A. Lewin

Illustrated by
ERNEST H. SHEPARD

available to all. Although this dream has never quite been fulfilled, there are still Esperanto societies throughout the world and people enthusiastically promoting it.

Even without such a systematic approach to word - and language - formation, we are always creating new words to fill holes in our vocabulary, or to express things for which we haven't yet found a proper dictionary entry. Perhaps there is a tendency in this age of innovation, research and discovery to believe that word creation is a specifically modern phenomenon, but every age has had its full complement of new words. Many, in fact, that we now think of as exclusively twentieth century phenomena came into being well before the last century began: *contact lens* dates from 1888, for example, *aeroplane* from 1873, *parachute* from 1785, *commuter* from 1865 and *homosexual* from 1894. Word creation - the official term is '*coining*' words or '*coinages*' - goes on all the time, naming new things, renaming old things, borrowing words from other languages, transferring them from one field of endeavour into another, slamming together bits of different existing words to create a new whole, or adapting existing words by adding prefixes (like *super-*) or suffixes (like-*orama*) to forge the new. Occasionally wordsmiths come up with original sets of phonemes that have never rubbed shoulders before to give lexical form to an idea previously undefined. Words like *blurb, quark* and *plip* are examples of this.

Flying machines had no equivalent precedent like cars had the horse and carriage, so new words had to be coined. France figured strongly in early aviation and many French words remain such as hangar, fuselage and aileron. Model of flying machine on view at the Science Museum, London.

But despite these fascinating historical early-risers, it is indisputable, as the lexicographer, John Ayto, who in 1999 compiled a dictionary of 'Twentieth Century Words', has pointed out, there has never been an age for coinages like the past one hundred years. More than 100,000 new terms were coined in that time, at least a thousand for each year of the century. This is an age unparalleled in human history simply because of the increase in population and the quickly changing fashions and needs which mass communication brings. And each decade, with its fascinations and fashions, naturally tended to reflect those preoccupations in the words it invented. So, to take one example, the 1900s which saw the advent of aviation, cars and the film business, were marked by *radiators, road signs, cameramen, airliners and hangars*. The name *Rolls Royce* has even become a commonly accepted adjective - as in phrases like 'we received *rolls royce* treatment'. But the same decade also coined words that quickly died the death, such as *hippomobile* (a 'horse-drawn vehicle' as opposed to motor-powered), *marconigram* - synonym for 'telegram' - and the confusing *saleing*, meaning shopping in the sales, which presumably collapsed under the weight of its own ambiguity.

Similarly, echoing the age they were coined in, are the wealth of war-related words from the decades that saw the First and Second World Wars and their build-up. Words like *blitz, torpedo, bombard, parachute* are now used in a variety of contexts. The youth culture in the 1950s and 60s also brought in new words, as did the space-race in the 1960s and 1970s and environmental and political correctness terminology in the 1980s.

From this neologising ferment of the twentieth century, it is worth taking a leap back one thousand years to Britain before the Norman Conquest. Many core terms were the

same in the separate dialects of Old English as they are in present day English, although subsequent changes in pronunciation may make their meaning opaque to the modern ear. To what degree did the people of Winchester, speaking their Wessex dialect at the seat of Saxon power, invent new words for ideas and objects that had previously never been named?

Compared with the English of four hundred years later in the Renaissance, spoken Old English has a tiny recorded vocabulary. A need arose to fill lexical gaps as they developed, particularly in the area of religion and theology. According to the Old English specialist, **Dr. Kathryn Lowe** of Glasgow University, English speakers of pre-Conquest days preferred to follow the model that their modern Germanic counterparts still practice, which is to form compound words from existing terms rather than by using loan words:

Back in the Middle Ages I think the options for lexical creation were limited: they could either choose to simply borrow the words from Latin into English wholesale, or they could use '*compounding*' or '*loan-translations*'. (Modern examples of compounds would include 'hatchback' and 'loudspeaker' - there are thousands of them!) And that's in fact what they chose to do, because the Anglo-Saxons were pretty resistant to the whole idea of borrowing. Only about three per cent of words in Old English are actually borrowings from different languages.

With all this talk of 'compounding' and 'loan-translation', it would perhaps be timely to identify the five different ways in which, according to linguists, coinages are created. As we have seen, the simplest way to fill a gap is to find a new use for a word that is already in the dictionary. Thus, the computer-builders of 1965 who were looking for a word to describe the mechanism they had manufactured for controlling the cursor-arrow on the screen, called it a *mouse* because its rounded form and tail-like cable vaguely resembled the familiar rodent. They also gave a new prominence to words like *menu*, *default* or *download* and built a whole new vision around the figurative use of words like *windows* and *apple*.

Another familiar process is to borrow an existing word from another language. As old as the English language itself, we saw this great blossoming during the Renaissance when 30,000 new words joined the language, as detailed in the first book of *The Routes of English*. But, it's a process that neither started nor ended then. Many

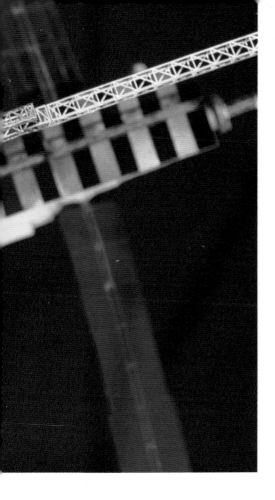

The Mir space station. In the Cold War Russia chose space as the battleground to beat the USA if nowhere else. So many terms are of Russian origin, such as sputnik, cosmonaut.

languages are today pressed into use. For instance, Japanese has given us *karaoke* ('empty orchestra') and native Australian has given us *budgerigar* ('good cockatoo'). A vast array of terms also continue to flow in from closer to home via, for example, politics and social phenomena - *sputnik, glasnost, perestroika* are three obvious Russian examples from the past forty years.

Compounding, as **Dr. Lowe** pointed out, was a phenomenon of Old English, but today it is the most familiar and commonest form of lexical creation. Thus from the *fridge-freezer* to *lap-dancing* we are combining existing words - *compounding* them together - to denote something specific and distinct from the compound's constituent parts.

Add to this the twentieth-century's own particular gift to the compounding process which linguists call *blending,* which is putting not just words together to denote something new, but merely **parts** of words. So helicopters land at *heliports* ('helicopter-airports') and travellers stop over at motels ('motor-hotels'). Students

Early clockmaking developed in France but England took it on in the seventeenth and eighteenth centuries. Parts are called by the French names rather than having English engineering terms. Not 'axle' but 'arbor' from the French 'arbre'; 'escarpement' from 'echappement'; 'pinion' from 'pignon'.

categorise universities as *Oxbridge* ('Oxford and Cambridge') or *redbrick* (which is a compound, rather than a blend) and may well consume *brunch* in preference to eating both breakfast and lunch. According to John Ayto, this penchant for blending may have developed from the Victorians' love of word-play, as characterised by the nonsense coinages of Lewis Carroll (*mimsy* is the example Ayto quotes). But, whatever the original impulse was, it is today a highly popular solution to the lexical gap.

A fifth way of coining new words is to shorten an existing word and create a new one. 'Abbreviation' is the technical term for this old-as-the-hills neologising technique. So centuries ago *grid* was formed from *gridiron*, and in the last hundred years, *destruct,* from *destruction*. Simpler than these so-called 'back-formations' were the manufactured abbreviations like *porn* from *pornography* and *fridge* from *refrigerator*. *Fridge* even modified its spelling to conform to existing words with similar pronunciations (*ridge, bridge, midge*) as did *marge* (from *margarine*).

As we have seen, the Old English period tended to rely upon forming compounds from existing words in order to designate new things or notions. But in 1066, as **Dr. Lowe** observes, all this would change.

After the Norman Conquest we see a complete change and much more readiness to take on board loan words - words borrowed from other languages - especially French. Our love affair with French started round about the thirteenth century and it hasn't really vanished. And I think the early Modern English period (the Renaissance) was head and shoulders above any other period before or since, as far as borrowing words is concerned.

At the end of the fourteenth century, the great English poet, Geoffrey Chaucer, was

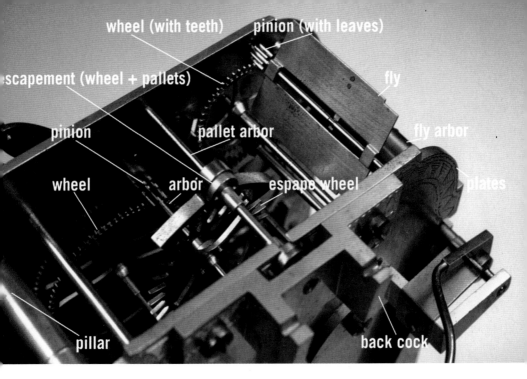

already filling his *Canon Yeoman's Tale* (in 'The Canterbury Tales') with what he called 'termes', technical vocabulary in this case to do with alchemy - over fifty of them altogether. Many of these words, not found elsewhere before this tale and thus considered examples of coinages, subsequently fell by the wayside, but others, such as *amalgam* live on to this day in words like the *amalgam* fillings dentists use or the verb to *amalgamate*.

The waves of borrowing from French after the Norman Conquest and from other European languages during the Renaissance constitute two of the most significant neologising eras of English. The rise of modern science and engineering in the seventeenth and eighteenth centuries also brought a massive wave of word-creation to serve the multitude of new discoveries and inventions, not to mention the modes and manners of fashionable London that developed during the same period. This was coining it in the modern manner.

Roy Porter is Professor of the History of Medicine at the Wellcome Institute and has made a special study of the growth of new scientific terms during this period:

A lot of it is to do with the discovery of the world. Suddenly you find that there are thousands of plants and elements and stars and things that nobody quite knows what to call. When, at the end of the eighteenth century, the astronomer William Herschel

The Cutty Sark, the fastest clipper bringing tea from China in the 1870s. As a leading maritime trading nation shipping was of crucial importance to Britain and several specific terms used then permeate ordinary language now. 'Learning the ropes', 'all clewed (clued) up', and 'going to the bitter end' started their linguistic life on board vessels such as the Cutty Sark.

discovered a new planet, he had to find a name. But what do you call a new planet? He wanted to call it 'George's Planet', after King George; that, however, was considered rather too vulgar, and... they worried that the French wouldn't like it very much if a whole planet was called after England. So, in the end, they latinised it, calling it 'Uranus' instead. It's a very, very delicate business exactly how you go about scientific naming.

In fact, **Professor Porter** points out the irony that the word *scientist* itself is quite a late arrival on the scene, dating from 1840, well after the surge in scientific interest began. Previously men who devoted themselves to such intellectual pursuits were known by the loan words *literati* or *savants* or *virtuosi*, while the word *intellectual* dates from about 1810. We borrowed French and Italian words because we didn't really have a word of our own.

Much of the scientific terminology that was coined in the seventeenth, eighteenth and nineteenth centuries was classical in origin, drawing heavily on Latin and Greek for suitable source-words. Already in the sixteenth century, the pre-eminence of Latin as a linguistic source had, as described in the first volume of *The Routes of English*, been the subject of furious debate amongst certain scholars. They raged over the fashionable attempt to introduce so-called 'Inkhorn' terms (essentially pedantic coinages based on Latin) to replace supposed vulgarisms. So the invented *deruncinate* was recommended to replace common-or-garden pruning and it was deemed more seemly to *carbunculate* an object than to simply burn it to cinders. Many scholars opposed these heavyweight newcomers, though some 'Inkhorn' inventions like *impede* and *dismiss* did survive to become part of our standard modern English.

But there was little dispute over the use of Latin and Greek for scientific coinages.

Abdomen, corolla, cortex, equilibrium, formula, genus, quantum, saliva, stamen, tibia and vertebra are but a handful of scientific coinages that have been drawn directly from Latin; while from Greek one can easily assemble a list including *anode, barometer, cathode, electrolysis, electron and zoology*. There are hundreds, if not thousands more. One of the curious factors that lies behind this penchant amongst scientists for the classical root is to do with what many see now as a certain intellectual snobbery.

Dr. Denis Smith, former lecturer in Engineering Science at the University of East London, joined the *Routes of English* team at the Science Museum in London to discuss scientific and engineering lexical creativity. Speaking in front of possibly the finest example of a textile mill steam engine - one of the great engineering creations of the age of steam - the Industrial Revolution - **Dr. Smith** was adamant that different geniuses drove scientists and engineers to coin words in different ways:

There is a cultural background to the way people come into the subject. I think the distinction is really that the scientists were always properly educated people; they would have been public schoolboys, would have gone to university, would probably have read the classics as well as studying science, which was already by the late eighteenth and early nineteenth centuries a university-level discipline including physics and chemistry. For engineers there was nowhere to go. You had to learn by apprenticeship, by pupillage to a well-known engineer, and you learned on the job. And this distinction governed the way scientists and engineers coined new words to fit their needs. So, the new engineering words were really rather more descriptive and graphic than the scientific.

Thus in the early Industrial Revolution engineers were looking at animals and the human

analogies (*fishplate, beetle, stress, strain and fatigue*), borrowing words that had been used in similar circumstances to try and explain engineering operations. I think it comes a bit later when the scientists start making an input into the engineering process.

And the educational status of these scientists bred a sort of intellectual arrogance. **Professor Roy Porter**:

It was one of the great claims of so many nineteenth century scientists when they were naming the elements that they weren't just scientists in the lab, but they were scholars of Greek or Latin. And therefore they were proud of themselves when they thought of words like '*palaeolithic*', instead of saying simply 'dawn of time'. '*Palaeolithic*' gave everything a kind of higher status.

Similarly, **Roy Porter** points out that when, around the turn of the nineteenth century, scientists needed to find a name for the new scientific study of rock structures and their development, they turned again to Latin to form *geology* (the study of the earth). As the new *geologists* identified the bedrock strata they were uncovering, again they had to find new names for them:

I've always been interested in how geological terms came into being, how you actually named the strata. How do you actually invent a vocabulary? One of the things that they did in Britain is to try to trade on particular sorts of local and historical and antiquarian associations, but in a very Latinate form. So when you found particular sorts of rocks in mid-Wales, instead of calling them 'slatey rocks' or 'grey rocks' or 'hard rocks' or 'friable rocks' or something like that, you called them *Silurian*. *Silurian* was based on the Latin name of the tribes who'd lived there - a word taken from the writings of Caesar.

Similarly, **Professor Porter** points out, *Cambrian* rocks were named after the Welsh and

Jasminum Arabicum
Lauri folio, cujus semen
apud nos Café dicitur,
Ac . R. Paris.

The first known illustration in Britain of the coffee plant, Coffea Arabica The term was originally Arabic, then entered the Turkish language, finishing finally in a latinised form in English.

Until the botanist and zoologist, Linnaeus published his 'Species plantarum' in 1753 plant naming was chaotic. Plants had many names and the same name often applied to several plants.

Note in the bottom lefthand part of the illustration the confusion which prevailed whilst trying to label the coffee plant. The botanist has named it several ways, including 'Jasminum Arabicum', though it is not nowadays classified as jasmine. He did acknowledge its origins in Arabia.

the *Permian* system in geology after a place in Russia called Perm:

It's right in the centre of the Urals. An English geologist was riding through the area, saw a new sort of rock, asked the locals what the place was called and discovered it was called Perm. Thus it became the *Permian* system. And there's something quaint and arbitrary and idiosyncratic and yet also pretentious about the way in which science goes about naming things.

It is not such a huge step from coinages with an academic flavour - like these that formally defined the expanding world of scientific enquiry - to the darker, shadier and decidedly shiftier world of the medical mountebank. The claims made by eighteenth-century quack doctors for their patent cure-alls are testimony to the supposed power of the newly fashionable pursuit of scientific study as well as to the richness of the linguistic inventive powers of the age. As **Roy Porter** says:

Neologisms are ways of selling anything and everything, and as a historian of medicine I find the language of quackery extremely interesting. Because quacks are the people who've actually got to have the gift of the gab and if they're selling anything it's presence and persona. There's a wonderful and well documented patter by a German quack doctor which was recorded by a journalist called Edward Ward at Tower Hill in London in the early eighteenth century. It's full of malapropisms as well as words to impress:

'... Gentlemen, I present to you with my 'Universal Solutive', which
corrects all the Cacochymick and Cachexical disease of the Intestines,
Hydrocephalous, Epileptick Fits, Flowing of the Gall and many other distempers not
hitherto distinguished by name... 'My Friendly Pills' called the Never Failing
Helogenes... operate seven several different ways, viz Hypnotically, Hydrotically,

Cathartically, Proppysinatically, Hydragoically, Pulmatically, and last Synecdochically, by corroborating the whole Oeconomia Animalis'.

Now you'd have bought his pills, wouldn't you?

The Routes of English team also visited the Royal Observatory at Greenwich in London, still today the very centre of world time, straddling as it does the Greenwich 0-degree meridian. Amongst the many fine timepieces from several centuries are the magnificent creations of that dazzling Leonardo of clock-creation, John Harrison. But Harrison is not the only, merely the most distinguished, of a whole series of British masterbuilders who took the genius of continental horology and made it their own during the seventeenth and eighteenth centuries. These men - and they were pretty well exclusively men at this time - were engineers of the finest detail, borrowing, adapting, creating afresh new designs and new principles. And the language they used to describe their skills and what they had used to build their artefacts was a perfect microcosm of the principle of linguistic coinage.

Here, therefore, you find borrowings - 'loan-translations' - from the earlier French craftsmen clock-builders: spindles in clocks are known not, as elsewhere in British engineering, as *axles* but as *arbors*, after the French term *arbre*, 'a tree', in this case, specifically an 'axle-tree'. Similarly, the device for meting out the small parts of time is known as an *escapement*, which is derived from the French *échappement* - literally an 'escape'.

When a British clockmaker needed to describe the moving parts of the mechanism, again, he unwittingly followed one of the fundamental principles of word coinage: he took an existing word and gave it a new specificity - just like the computer designers invented the *mouse*. Only the horologists put *snails* in their clocks, to regulate the number of strokes a clock will chime - a tiny part shaped very like the curled up shape of a snail. They also used *worms* which were helical screws that twisted a little like a worm, and *flies* to regulate the spinning of the chiming mechanism, a sort of airbrake that whirred and buzzed rather like a frustrated fly. In taking analogies from the animal kingdom, the clockmakers were following a very sound engineering principle, for, as we have already established, engineers tended to call things by names that were clearly descriptive of their shape or function, whereas the scientists, burdened with their classical education, preferred to draw upon their erudition. **Jonathan Betts**, the Curator of Horology at the Royal Observatory, is a passionate student of time and timekeepers and also of the language the clockmakers employed:

In the Age of Enlightenment, academics and gentlemen dilettantes liked to introduce new terms in the language to express the new technology, because they felt it empowered those new objects with a certain cachet and set them apart from the rest. For example, when John Arnold, the great chronometer-maker made his highly successful Chronometer Number Thirty Six, (which before that time would have been referred to as a *timekeeper*), he and his sponsor, the Hydrographer of the Navy, Alexander Dalrymple, said '*this device is far better than anything that's gone before. We must emphasise this by giving it a new name*'. So from the Greek they invented the term *chronometer* - (from *chronos* meaning *time* and *metron*, 'a measure') 'timekeeper', if you like. And thus the term *chronometer* is entirely invented, very much a product of the eighteenth century, and typical of this penchant for concocting pseudo-classical terms for newly-invented objects.

Interestingly, many of the first craftsmen working in steam previously worked materials on a miniature scale, as clock-builders. And so, in time-honoured neologising

practice, when they required a term to describe the moving parts of a steam-driven mechanism, they re-employed the words they already knew. **Jonathan Betts** described this:

Many of the Spinning Jennies that Richard Arkwright had built for his mills were constructed by clockmakers. And the 'wheels' they used, of course, were referred to as such with the 'teeth' and the 'pinions', the 'leaves' and 'pivots' and so on, all directly from horology. There was no other engineering technology before horology except, arguably millwork, but then that was on a very much larger scale, so it was naturally the clockmakers and turret clockmakers that the engineers looked to when they wanted these machines made.

But soon afterwards very specific mechanisms began to appear which were not related to clock-making. There's very little in the detail of steam engines, for example, which is common to clockwork, and so they quickly began to develop vocabularies of their own. But the clockmakers were at the root of it, for sure.

And what did they do when they wanted new words for steam? In true engineering fashion, and in contrast to the Latinising scientists, they borrowed analogies from the world they knew. So they developed *beetles* for hammering, *rams* for giving things a hefty thump. **Dr. Denis Smith**, writer and lecturer in Engineering and Technology, has a favourite:

The one I like best is when the iron manufacturer, Abraham Darby at Coalbrookdale, first produced his smelted iron ore using coke rather than charcoal, a new word came into the language. The process of tapping the blast furnace and casting the molten iron into little blocks on the foundry floors produced long runs and branch runs and then further little

branches. Can you imagine that? But when former agricultural workers came into the iron industry, the first thing they said was that this shape reminded them of a sow lying down, being suckled by her piglets. And so the term 'pig iron' was born - a word which is now part of the language and which had pure animal origins.

Another very good example is the term 'horsepower', which had to be invented because if you were trying to sell somebody a new-fangled steam engine in the second half of the eighteenth century, the chap who was buying it would want to know how many horses it would replace. So there was this mechanical/animal equivalence that came in, devised by James Watt, which amounted to the average amount of work a horse could do by lifting a weight out of a well over a pulley and walking away from the well-head. Watt experimented with lots of different horses and came to an average figure. And that became a measure, and known as 'horsepower'.

As we have seen, the most common forms of word-coinage are in fact reappropriation of existing words - like 'pig', above. Although arguably, the coinage *pig iron* designated something completely new and, in fact, had only the most tenuous connection with its porcine origins. But the area of word-creation that seems most to fascinate today are the words that come from nowhere - the absolute beginners of the lexicon. As John Ayto has pointed out in his 'Twentieth Century Words', such 'root-creations' as they are known, created *ex nihilo*, represent less than one percent of coinages, and yet by their very strangeness and unfamiliarity they exercise a tremendous hold on the imagination. Lewis Carroll, with his wealth of strange nonsense words (some in fact compounds, like *slithy* = 'slimy' and 'lithe') or James Joyce, writing in his linguistically ground-breaking novel 'Finnegan's Wake' of *quarks*, (subsequently borrowed to describe sub-atomic particles), knew the powerful hold

that such coinages have on the imagination. This is the territory of poets and linguistic *imagineers* (a Hollywood neologism describing computer special effects creators, which could have a useful resonance beyond the film world!) and for such word-people, the resonances of good root-creations can embed them in the public's imagination, and, thus, in their lexicon.

In the 1990s men and women go and exist in the self-sufficient sealed world of the *biosphere*, and if we no longer clamour at the butcher's for *kesp* (artificial meat-type Spun Protein) we still clean the carpet with a *hoover*. We cannot pick up a book without finding a *blurb* on the back cover (invented in 1907 by the American humorist Gelett Burgess). Often objects have official names which are either generally unknown or too unwieldy to gain currency and a root-creation can spring up amongst users that eventually catches on.

For *The Routes of English*, we carried out some informal research into the spread of understanding of the word *plip*, used by car-manufacturers to describe the infra-red remote control device that opens central-locking systems. The word is presumably descriptive, vaguely onomatopoeic, echoing the clunking noise of the operation, and is to be found in car manuals (*'plip,* remote control locking unit....' 'when the doors have been unlocked using the *plip...*' Renault User Manual 1997). Yet it clearly has still limited currency as several well-known lexicographers of current usage as well as non-specialists consulted had no knowledge of the term.

In a similar area, where the official term for a recent invention in widespread use is cumbersome and ugly, there is often huge linguistic inventiveness in the home, with many evocative, funny and effective neologisms in everyday use. Thus, a 'remote control device' which accompanies TV and videos is often described as a *zapper* - not elegant, and with few evocative or humorous resonances, but an effective and well-rooted word with appropriate associations (ZAP! from comic-books - Ayto dates it to 1929 - and its transferred meaning of to 'hit energetically', thus to *zap* from channel to channel on TV).

This process that sees the gradual embedding and general acceptance of a neologism is going on all the time. The rapid growth in use of the Internet, personal computers and of electronic communication in the last five years is reflected in the acceptance of the coinages associated with them. **Elizabeth Knowles**, a lexicographer with the Oxford English Dictionaries, talked about her work editing the Oxford Dictionary of New Words:

When we were preparing the text for 'New Words' people were still talking about '*electronic mail*' and the verbal form - to e-mail - was less common. It was certainly there, it was certainly important, but it hadn't taken over to anything like the degree it has now. That was something which really exploded, to a point where people now look for an e-mail address as a matter of course. Somebody will say, '*Oh I'll e-mail you about that*', or '*Are you*

on e-mail?' The other person might say *'No I'm not'*; but they're not going to say, *'What do you mean?'* It's something which has now become completely familiar within the language.

But coinages have their 'sell-by dates' too. Some new terms arrive quickly, maybe on the coat tails of a news event or fashion-craze, and fade equally quickly:

It's always interesting to look at the words which have had a very high profile at a particular moment, relating to a particular news story, and seeing whether they survive. '*Twigloo*' is an interesting word: it's a structure made up of twigs and branches, in which people can live and camp, which came to prominence during the protests over the building of the Newbury Bypass. It's made up of a blend of 'igloo', 'twig', and it's really quite a nice word. But how long will it last? If road protests and their encampments disappear, it will be interesting to see whether in five years you find any further references to that particular word.

After the Falklands War, the term *yomp* was briefly very much used for describing going across very difficult terrain, it's a Marine term originally, I think, so it would initially have been used among them, but it would not have been used, or understood, in the outside world. Then we had the Falklands War when there was a lot of direct reporting, and quite suddenly, a word which has been part of a special vocabulary set moves out into the wider world. It's still known, it's in dictionaries, but I don't think there's anything like the common use of it, and I don't think it's one of those words which really made the transition into being a generally used word.

Slang and its fast-moving lexicon of neologisms accounts for many of the most popular new words today. This, though, is a class of coinages so transitory that they barely reach the dictionary. But, as far as *spoken* English is concerned, they more than simply exist: they are emblematic; they are like designer labels, defining the user as

one of the gang - or altogether out of it.

One such is 'wicked'. 'Wicked' has for some time signified 'terrific', 'fantastic' for children and teenagers, yet so widespread has it now become that it has lost much of its currency. Today, wicked is too common to be fashionable; just as its 1960s' equivalents 'swinging' and 'dodgy' fell out of fashion and disappeared as quickly as did flared jeans. Yet it is not so long since **Professor Roy Porter's** first encounter with the 'wicked' seal of approval:

About five years ago, I got back a student questionnaire I'd sent out evaluating the work I was doing. And the person had written, '*this guy's lectures are wicked*'. Now I know what '*wicked*' means nowadays, but at the time I thought I was about to be prosecuted!

The prize-winning novelist and poet, **Helen Dunmore**, shares **Roy Porter's** relish for this sort of usage:

I'm interested in the use of opposites as with 'wicked'; I like the idea of 'bad' and 'good' being transposed, 'it's bad' - another piece of street-speak. And I think that is part of the elitism of language, of having this little sealed glass bell jar of language, which you and your friends and your intimates revel in - it could be a management group, a group of computer technicians or a group of kids on the street corner. And it's that revelling and pleasure in the language that I think people enjoy so much. They love language and want to savour words in their mouths.

Dr. Kathryn Lowe also has a particular current slang neologism she favours:

The new one seems to be '*it's gone pants*'. That's so descriptive, such a lovely phrase, that I've started using it myself, much to my colleagues' dismay, I think!

Finally, we turn to those whose trade is neologising, who earn their living by making up, dreaming up, new words and names for products, catching the fashionable wind and using it to drive sales, branding and market penetration. **Simon Luke** is head of the Naming Team at a company called Interbrand, Newell and Sorrell and many of the coinages they invent, (the biscuit *Hob-nobs* and the anti-depressant drug *Prozac* were named by them) which were created purely with a commercial purpose, have become fully-fledged lexical items that now turn up routinely in dictionaries. He talked about his work:

You need to have a differentiated name as well as a well known name. Brand names that become generic and end up in the dictionary, like *Hoover* and *Sellotape*, are examples where people might well mistake other products for those brands. That's quite good for Hoover and Sellotape because it means their names are getting out there, but it's also quite bad because it means they're also selling products for other people.

And there are many famous examples of names, or words, if you like, that were once trademarks that now everyone uses freely - names like *zip*, which used to be a trademark, *escalator* used to be a trademark and so on but everyone uses it now as a descriptor. And that is the danger if you let things get out of hand.

In the early 1970s, the American pharmaceutical company Eli Lilly developed a new drug product which was highly effective in combating depressive conditions in humans. The compound's chemical name was *fluoxetine hydrochloride*. But no pharmaceutical manufacturer is allowed to own exclusively a formal chemical designation. So, to market *fluoxetine*, Lilly Industries turned to the wordsmiths of Interbrand:

The role of the name was to establish very quickly the product as a byword for a particular emotional experience, and the emotional experience was 'makes you feel better'. Given that we couldn't make *fluoxetine* a trademark, our starting point was from zero. So the first thing we did was talk to our client about the sort of name they wanted that product to have: if you wanted to suggest positivity you might pick something like a sun, or some type of natural imagery might have worked. But maybe that approach would have seemed somewhat trivialising for this product and maybe too it wouldn't have worked in more than one language - there are many words for 'sun', for example. So you then move to a position

Kodak. Where on on earth did such a distinctive and eminently suitable word come from? George Eastman pulled it out of the air in 1888 when he introduced the Kodak camera to the world. 'K' was his favourite letter being strong and incisive so he put it at both ends of the word. Like 'Prozac' and 'Häagen-Dazs', what sounds right, is right.

where you realise that there isn't perhaps an existing dictionary word in any language that would be appropriate, and maybe we need to invent this word.

We then began to have discussions about what this word should suggest, and one of the core benefits of *fluoxetine* was positivity, so we realised that *pro* (signifying 'for' and 'forwards' in Latin, as in 'proceed') was a prefix that had connotations and suggestions of positivity and that worked in many languages.

Then we also wanted the word to be quite hi-tech and modern because this was a new breed of drugs. Silly though it sounds, letters like '*z*' weren't very much used in pharmaceutical branding when we were working on this fifteen years ago. So we looked at '*z*'s and we looked at '*x*'s and we looked at '*y*'s, and that's how we got to '*zac*'.

To cut a long story short, '*zac*' is a bit like '*attack*' - it's attacking a problem - and it's got the '*z*' which sounds very zippy and fast and was little used in pharmaceutical branding at the time. We slowly came to assemble the word-parts and the letters, and *Prozac* was the one that came through. And the proof is in the pudding: *Prozac*'s actually now in the dictionary.

So a new word enters the lexicon. A new star is born. Linguistic coinage is indeed a process with a magical quality to it. It is creating gold from nothing. It is a process with a direct line to the babblings of childhood; a time when words can take whatever form you please, when sounds can mean anything you like, when 'cat' can mean 'dog' and when you can decide to invent a language called *Lalpen* just because you like muesli and the sound the word makes.

But, if **Simon Luke** and his colleagues earn considerable sums for making up *Prozac*

and *Hob-nobs* and the like, the naming of parts is just as effective and memorable when the new word falls fully-formed, like a meteorite from nowhere, like *pig iron* or *gospel.* The magic is of the new; it is the pleasure, as the poet **Helen Dunmore** says, of having these neologisms in one's mouth, trying them out, putting them in a sentence and seeing how they work in practice. It is the exhilaration of flying solo.

And, given good soil and favourable growing conditions, the coinage will take root and, as **Elizabeth Knowles** of the Oxford Dictionary of New Words observes, become a fully grown member of the lexicon:

To become naturalised, a new coinage gradually functions more and more like any other word. If it's a noun, a verb might be formed from it; it might then acquire suffixes, so perhaps adjectives or adverbs can be formed; it may combine with other words and, in the end perhaps in every respect, it will operate like any other word. At that point, its origin will be interesting in that it's part of its etymology, but the word will have its own life in English.

LANGUAGE AT PLAY

What makes a good joke? Is it the situation? Or maybe the punchline? Or is it the knock-em-over, falling-about-pleasures of good slapstick? The chances are that whatever the humour is , unless we are talking about mime artists like Marcel Marceau or the great Jacques Tati, there are going to be words in it somewhere. They are at the very heart of what makes us laugh. What has made the English split their side over the centuries has been the comedy of words.

This is Ronnie Barker, one of the most popular comedians of the last fifty years, in serious appeal-to-the-nation mode, looking straight at the camera:

I am the secretary for the *Loyal* Society for the Relief of Sufferers from *Pissmonunciation*... (big laughs) and the reason I am once more *squeaking* to you tonight...(more laughter). is that many people last time couldn't understand what I was spraying. So here I am back again on your little *queens* to strain it and make it all *queer* for you.(hysterical laughter and applause).

Wit, puns, spoonerisms, even inaccurate ones like Ronnie's, play-on-words, silly suggestive names, double entendres, malapropisms, good word jokes, bad word jokes, the BBC air waves have been filled with the sound of people playing with language. In the final series of Rowan Atkinson's celebrated TV comedy, Blackadder has only to address the hapless Captain Darling, without crediting him with his full title, for the audience to fall about:

> **Blackadder:** *What do you want, Darling?*
> **Darling:** *It's Captain Darling to you...*

They never tire of the joke. This sort of double entendre is as old as language itself. It is one of the many forms of linguistic misunderstanding based on confusing one word with another that sounds the same. Shakespeare was not above making his Frenchmen pronounce the word *third* in habitual manner without the '*h*', and gets a cheap laugh every time. And in 'Much Ado About Nothing', Beatrice calls Count Claudio '...*(as) civil as an orange*' - the sort of pun that would make today's, and I suspect sixteenth-century, audiences groan at its ludicrous approximation (*civil* sounding *Seville*, where the oranges come from). A good contemporary pun, the fruit - and the neologism *orange* that was imported with it - arrived on Britain's shores about a hundred or so years before Shakespeare was writing. And there's a little linguistic curiosity here too: *a norange* was originally closer in sound to the *naranja* of Spain, but the word division appears to have shifted over time. It's an example of the way words change, enriching the game of playing with language.

Professor Walter Redfern of the University of Reading, who has written a book about puns, believes that:

Word-play has to do with lateral thinking, the ability to suddenly bifurcate, to spring across a gap like a spark. This is all to do with intelligence, (though not education - anyone can do it). Word play is economical: you can say something in a much shorter space and much shorter time by a pun or by some other form of wordplay than you can if you had to spell it all out.

Homophones (words that sound alike), homonyms (words that mean the same), alliteration, assonance (the repetition of sounds) and rhyme all come to the aid of the punster, the man or woman who likes to play with words. And, ultimately, that is what we are talking about when we refer to verbal jokes. It's all language play, the cut and thrust of meaning and morphology, of word-shape and word-sound. For most of us it is completely without material purpose, so why do so many of us do it?

According to **Professor David Crystal**, author of many authoritative works on language and

compiler of the 'Cambridge Encyclopaedia of the English Language', people play with language for a whole range of different reasons. Some do it because they simply want a good laugh and the play of the moment gives them that possibility. Other people play with words because they are fascinated with language and want to explore its potential for variation and creativity. Yet others do it because they feel competitive and want to beat somebody at this business of getting to grips with language and being in control over it.

There are all sorts of different reasons. I suppose the bottom line is that people play with language because it's there, and whenever you're faced with something as intricate and complex and as fascinating as language, you want to get the most out of it.

Playing with words is a natural human activity, from the first babblings of a child taking his or her first steps in language, to the normal to and fro of conversation at the dinner table. **David Crystal** recalls one such moment:

One of the occasions I remember very well was when somebody referred to their cat meeting a neighbour's cat in the middle of the road. And, quick as a flash, one of the people in the group said, '*Oh there was a cat-frontation*', obviously based on '*confrontation*'. Now that might have been left there, but it wasn't. The other people in the group started to chip in. One of them said '*Oh that was a cat-astrophe*', and then someone else said, '*Oh that was a cat-alyst for further meetings*', and somebody else said, '*Oh but one of the cats wasn't very*
42

Recording session of 'Round the Horne', one of
Radio 4's most pioneering comedy programmes of
the 1960s which played with regional accents,
double entendre and innuendo. The title itself was
a triple entendre!

well: she had cat-arrh'.

**And so the joke went bouncing around until people got fed up with it or simply ran out of
words beginning with 'cat'. At that point, the conversation goes back onto an even keel until
someone else makes another comment which generates another pun and the cycle goes
round again.**

This sort of 'ping-pong punning' as it is sometimes known, is a familiar human phenomenon,
amongst people who have only just met almost as much as amongst old friends. People indulge
in word play, according to **Professor Crystal**, as a good way of beginning to knot the bonds of
friendship. And the benchmark of approval amongst the assembled company is usually not the
traditional chortle but a groan; the bigger the groan, the more successful the pun.

Language play, then, is a form of *passepartout,* a clever form of social interaction that allows us
to establish contact across a common ground. And professional comics trade on this
universality - approximately half the game shows on radio and television are language-based -
when they too indulge in wordplay.

David Crystal again:

**With language play you can pretty well guarantee that the people you're talking to will
recognise what you're doing when you are treating a normal piece of language in an unusual
way, twisting it, making a joke with it. And this can pretty well guarantee that the people
you're talking to will recognise what you're doing because they've done precisely the same
things themselves on another occasion. The only difference is that they haven't been paid
for it whereas as the professional comic has. I suppose it's one of those things that accounts
for why language games are so common on radio and television.**

So, if it is so natural a part of human behaviour to play around with words, make puns and

Mr and Mrs Discobbolos. An illustration by Leslie Brooke from 'The Pelican Chorus' and other nonsense verses by Edward Lear. Edward Lear was both an artist and a writer of children's nonsense verse. 'A Book of Nonsense', published in 1845 was immediately popular in the Victorian nursery and has remained so to the present day. His most famous poems include 'The Owl and the Pussycat' and 'The Jumblies' which children love for their rhythm and linguistic invention and for the quality of their fantasy. The poems are, however, tinged with the melancholy from which Lear suffered throughout his life.

using double meanings to raise at least a smile, where do we get the habit from? One thing is certain, we like to copy each other as **David Crystal's** ping-pong punning example above illustrates. Also some are better at doing it than others: the ability to recognise, enjoy and then put into practice the delicious ambiguities of *tier* and *tear*, *pair* and *pear*, *pier* and *peer,* for example, is not given to all in equal measure. Yet there is no doubt that the enjoyment of words and playing with them begins early on in our lives.

Back in the 1980s, **Carol Fox**, a Senior Lecturer at the University of Brighton, recorded children telling stories at home, often when they did not know they were being recorded. Then she analysed the forty-nine thousand words that made up this junior tale-telling and made some fascinating discoveries about the way young people enjoy inventing and using nonsense words, rhyme and assonance:

The stories included verses and poems and pretend news broadcasts and weather forecasts. I was really surprised by how incredibly creative the children were with words, particularly, inventing their own terms and often indulging in a kind of phonological sound-play. There were lots of rhymes, lots of inversions of sounds such as you get in the works of Edward Lear or Spike Milligan. Five-year-old Sundari was particularly competent at this kind of word play, especially rhyme. For instance, the names for the children in one of her stories are '*Truggle* and *Muggle*', and the tale is called *Double Muddle, Toil and Trouble*. She loves rhymes; she loves the sounds of silly words, and what is going on is sheer pleasure and fun - sheer entertainment value - for Sundari.

On another occasion, **Carol Fox** taped the young Sundari's reaction to an Edward Lear poem about the '*quangal wangal quee*' which sets the girl off on a feast of word-juggling:

She made up a whole story using the '*qu*' sounds - I think it was *quoggly-woggly trees* that she started with, and managed to sustain quite a long narrative where nearly all the nouns

were a kind of inverted sound play and word play of this type. Then, again, in an invented verse recorded by her mother when she was six years old and after I'd finished collecting all her narratives, she extemporises a whole poem where she experiments with using the '*r*' sound at the front of every word, immensely enjoying the sounds of the names '*Robert*' and '*Rinky*'. The effect is that it becomes incredibly abstract and bizarre. It doesn't necessarily make semantic sense, but it makes a kind of '*nonsense-sense*' of its own.

Carol Fox thinks that, at this stage in their development, children are freed from the regularising effects of formal meaning and the need to communicate in a very direct manner and are prepared to take risks with language:

I think they're doing that because they want their storytelling to seem impressive and to sound right. We have one pretend news-broadcast which starts: '*In Australia there has been a failure*', and I'm not sure that the child concerned actually knew what '*a failure*' was, but he was absolutely delighted with the rhyme that he'd made and with the way it sounded - very news-like. And, of course, he would quickly have acquired the word '*failure*' as time went on. In another story, Sundari uses a favourite word, which was '*weary*'. She introduces a character and says: '*her name was a weary name called Donna*'. And later on in the same story she sings a whole song using the word '*weary*' in which she turns the adjective into a verb - to '*wear*'. That kind of syntactic transference goes on all the time in the storytelling.

So for **Carol Fox's** five-year-olds playing with language was as natural and as uninhibited as

A late seventeenth century woodcut enacting the old conflict of who wears the trousers. Even if men and women could not read the text that was printed alongside they would have recognised the humour. There were many ideas and jokes in circulation in the seventeenth century which did not match the patriarchal ideal of proverbs such as 'a man of straw is worth a woman of gold.' Humour about the sexes flourished in oral traditions, such as rhymes, ballads, folklore, and in print. Here is a joke from a 'Collection of the Choicest Joques and Repartees...' in 1684:

A married man told his wife that she could call nothing her own, but her hair-lace and Fillet, and that her very breech was not her own; which the harmless creature understanding, let something drop in the Bed one night that was not very odiferous; her Husband asking the reason of it, she answered, that whilst her Breech was her own she had command of it, but now it was his, she could not command that which belonged to another.

The message of jokes like this is that women were in charge of the domestic domain and men should really give up any idea of having authority there too. The derogatory label '*cotquean*' was given to men who meddled with women's business. Ballads like 'The Woman to the Plow and the Man to the Hen-Roost' (a popular song in 1629) portray the calamities which could happen in a family if the husband took charge of household affairs.

breathing, or, according to **Professor David Crystal**, as mother's milk:

The kind of language that becomes normal for you in the first year of life is very much a language of play. Consequently, not surprisingly, when you yourself start to use language you will also start to play with language. It becomes part of the basic fabric of your linguistic existence.

If it is as natural as breathing to play with language, it follows that the English language has been open to its possibilities since it grew into a coherent tongue. Of course, as we found in the first book of *The Routes of English*, the evidence for *spoken* English in the earliest years of the second millennium is virtually nil. And since wit - language play - most clearly resides in the word on the tongue first and foremost, our assumptions have to be based on a certain amount of conjecture. The monk Aelfric's *Colloquy*, written for the young novices in Wessex in the years leading up to the end of the tenth century, is our best guide as to the flavour of the spoken English of the time. It is, to say the least, light on puns. So we must extrapolate from the 'garglings' of Carol Fox's infant witnesses and assume that the words in the mouths of the ancient Anglo-Saxons were played with as freely as they are by today's youngsters.

But **Dr. Kathryn Lowe** of Glasgow University, a specialist in Old English, believes that there are pointers to be found in the literature that has reached us from the years before 1066. Her evidence is the popularity of the riddle as a literary style, of which over ninety examples have survived:

You have to remember that Anglo Saxon verse is oral and they really, really loved their riddles; there are all sorts of different types: you might have one, for example, where the subject is compared with a living creature of some kind. It could be an animal, often it's a person or it might be a plant. So a *goblet of wine* might be compared to a *beautiful woman: mad, bad, dangerous to know*, that kind of thing, something that leads you into temptation.

Then again, there are riddles where the subject is compared with an inanimate object; for example, a *sword* might be compared with *treasure*. Here too there are many possibilities for word-play.

And then, of course, you've got every schoolboy's favourite, the erotic group, where you've got a double meaning with a rather risqué solution and then a less salacious one. For example: Q: *what is a rising and boneless object that is grabbed and covered by a woman?* A: *dough for bread.*

Further evidence that our Anglo-Saxon-speaking ancestors enjoyed indulging in a bit of verbal cut and thrust comes from the way the writers manipulate the words they have at their disposal. The Old English vocabulary was relatively small, unswelled as it still was by the influences of French and Renaissance expansion that would follow over the next three centuries. Using their relatively meagre vocabulary resources, the Old English poets would create words by what is known as compounding, latching together existing words to form new

A satirical drawing from the nineteenth century lampooning the coarse style of speech of randy fishwives at Billingsgate.

Note the double entendre of 'de German sausage' and the puns on 'cod' and on 'sole'.

ones that would render a slightly different meaning. **Dr. Lowe** said:

I've counted sixty-four different words for 'battle'. Well over half of those only occur in poetry and they're compounds of this nature. To take an imaginary example: a *gar*, for instance is a 'spear' - put that together with *plega*, meaning 'play', 'exercise' to form *garplega* and it would mean 'spear-play' or 'battle'. It's a perfectly good compound which isn't actually recorded in Old English, but almost certainly would have been recognised by Anglo Saxons as a proper one. So it's quite clear that Anglo Saxons are making things up and enjoying the feel and the sound of the language. All of this makes me think that part of what went on at medieval feasts was a lot of word play, a lot of carousing and formal, very public, carefully-structured verbal cut-and-thrust, and I think you'd have found an Anglo-Saxon feast to be a most entertaining and interesting experience!

Alliteration is also an important feature of Old English literature, which would again indicate a readiness to use the way words resonate and chime with one another on the tongue.

Following the Norman Conquest, the influence of French on English was one of a number of fundamental changes that the language was to undergo. *Mercian,* the Midlands dialect of Old English that developed as the standard during the fourteenth and fifteenth centuries, gradually saw the inflexional endings, which indicated the function of the word in the sentence, fall away. So the verb forms 'I speak' and 'we speak' would no longer have distinctive endings which marked them as either first person singular or plural. Middle English, as used by Geoffrey Chaucer and his contemporaries, was already a language infinitely richer in resources with which to play than the language had been one or two hundred years previously. And even a casual knowledge of 'The Canterbury Tales' reveals a degree of word play and linguistic irony that is one of the work's principal pleasures. Add to this the thousands of words that began to arrive through the Court initially and then subsequently via the explosion of learning and travel that was ushered in by the Renaissance and, as **Professor David Crystal** observes, suddenly the language now has resources to play with unlike anything it had had before:

Take, for instance, some of these groups of words that we now have in the language which come from different sources like an Anglo Saxon word, a French word and a Latin word - words like *kingly*, *royal* and *regal*. As soon as you get triplets and doublets like that then, of course, it's just waiting for somebody to come in and play with them.

By the time of Britain's greatest literary user of English, William Shakespeare, to use language for wit and as a sort of verbal counterpart to dashing apparel and flashing swordplay was considered one of the essential attributes of the Elizabethan courtier. **Professor Peter Holland** of Birmingham University runs the Shakespeare Institute at Stratford-on-Avon and is steeped in this world of linguistic parry-and-thrust. He says this enjoyment of language went far beyond simply being able to speak effectively and grammatically. It was a genuine taking of pleasure in punning, double-meanings and general wordplay. But Shakespeare's interest in and

observation of language amongst different groups of Elizabethan society, he says, goes much further than the world of courtly wit:

The one thing that Shakespeare is able to do, above anybody else, is to hear what everybody is trying to say, to listen to a language that is being used by an aristocrat or by a worker - or by anybody in between. One of the things that people seem to enjoy doing on stage is *insulting people*. And the way you insult somebody is not only by saying something terribly familiar, but by producing massive lists of insults, as if the sheer quantity of language will itself be the stuff that will destroy your opponent.

In 'King Lear', the Earl of Kent verbally attacks Oswald whom he mocks as too much of a willing servant of Lear's enemies, calling him:

'A knave, a rascal, an eater of broken meats, a base, proud, shallow, beggarly, three-suited, hundred pound, filthy, worsted stocking knave, a lily-liver'd, action-taking knave, a whoreson, glass-gazing super-serviceable, finical rogue; one-trunk-inheriting slave; one that wouldst be a bawd, in a way of good service, and art nothing but the composition of a knave, beggar, coward, pandar, and the son and heir of a mongrel bitch'.

Peter Holland observes:

Whenever I've heard modern audiences listening to that, they've laughed - immediately, happily, joyfully - at the way this list goes on and on until Oswald just vanishes behind the insults! There's a lovely moment in 'Love's Labour's Lost' when two characters give the comic character (Shakespeare calls him 'a clown') called Costard, letters to carry, and each tips him. The first person gives him the money and says, '*There is remuneration*'. Costard

has no idea what the word '*remuneration*' means, so he looks at the money: '*Remuneration,*' he says, '*O! that's the Latin word for three farthings: three farthings, remuneration. What's the price of this? One penny. No, I'll give you a remuneration! Remuneration! Why, it is a fairer name than French crown*'. He enjoys the word, he loves it; it has come over into Costard's vocabulary and he's excited by the sheer way he's now got a label to attach to a sum of money.

One of the other things that can produce rich comedy for Shakespeare is a kind of malapropism *avant la lettre*. And for Shakespeare there is no better vehicle for this sort of laughing-stock language-dunce than the figure of the constable. Maybe the combination of authority and dull-wittedness appealed to his sense of fun, but, whatever the reason, as **Peter Holland** observes, Shakespeare seems recurrently to think that constables can't get their words straight. So the constable, Elbow, in 'Measure for Measure', repeatedly uses the wrong term, and in one instance, makes great play with the word 'respected', mistaking it for and misusing it as 'suspected':

'*The time is yet to come*', *says Elbow about his wife*, '*that she was ever respected with man, woman or child. I respected with her before I was married to her. If ever I was respected with her or her with me, let not Your Worship think me the poor Duke's officer.*'

Professor Holland comments:

It's a very simple joke but it happens over and over again in Shakespeare and it seems to be a rich source of comedy, just enjoying the sense that somebody reaches for a language just beyond their grasp, goes for something a little more dignified than they are, and ends up falling flat on their nose as a result.

One of the great things that Shakespeare scholarship has done in the last twenty years, according to **Peter Holland**, has been to uncover a lot of Shakespeare's dirty jokes:

And it's particularly there when people are often apparently terribly polite. There's a moment in 'Love's Labours Lost' where a male character says to a woman, '*Goodnight sweet owl*'. However we know now that '*owl*' in the period could be pronounced to rhyme with '*bowl*' - in fact it's a pun on '*vagina*' - he's saying '*Goodnight sweet hole*'. But it's a joke that editors were deaf to for centuries and audiences are still totally deaf to, but which was there in the richness of the way in which a word could suddenly creep across into another kind of meaning, without an audience necessarily realising what had happened.

My hypothesis is that Shakespeare only ever has a joke because he assumes that an audience will get it, and a successful writer like Shakespeare knows, (with increasing accuracy, as his career goes on) whether the audience will hear the double meaning or not. And if they don't hear the double meaning there's not much point in the joke and hence you don't bother.

But today's audience doesn't any longer catch the double meaning; it's lost the language. For an audience now, for a reader of the text, the jokes need to be spelled out in the footnotes, and there's nothing that kills a joke faster than spelling it out.

Others have been less welcoming to word play than Shakespeare. In the radio programme on the subject, **Melvyn Bragg** quoted an American dictionary as defining a pun as 'a form of wit to which wise men stoop and fools aspire' - hardly a warm welcome into the language, he commented! But, as **David Crystal** pointed out, literary opinions were often divided:

Dryden called puns (he referred to them as '*clinches*') '*the lowest and most grovelling form of wit*'. Yet, not so long later Charles Lamb was so pleased with puns, he actually wrote one of his essays entirely about them, lauding them to the skies and thinking these are the most

wonderful things that bring everyone together.

David Crystal believes that while some may claim to dislike wit, it is not so much language play to which they are objecting as the specific form it takes. Everyone needs, he claims, to burn off the 'ludic energy', the sort of electric charge of word-energy that each of us possesses and is born with, and that Carol Fox's little girl witness, Sundari, demonstrated so effectively:.

So, in Victorian times, for instance, many people who used to go on record as saying 'I hate puns' would nonetheless devise quite sophisticated language games which were more intellectual in content.

Lewis Carroll introduced wordgames around the turn of the century and the famous Victorian wordsmiths had competitions (which even the Royal family used to enter) in which they would, for example, construct a story in which every word began with the same letter of the alphabet, or a sonnet in which every word had the same vowel. And you get some extraordinarily wonderful constructions as in the work of C.C. Bombaugh. He was a Victorian wordsmith who constructed many poems with just one vowel in every word, like:

> *'Idling I sit in this mild twilight dim,*
> *Whilst birds, in wild, swift vigils, circling skim.*
> *Light winds in sighing sink, till, rising bright,*
> *Night's Virgin Pilgrim swims in vivid light'*

featuring only '*i*'s, or '*No cool monsoons blow soft on Oxford dons, orthodox, jog-trot bookworm Solomons'* using the letter '*O*' for every word and telling a great truth about Oxford Dons by the way in the process.

Lewis Carroll or Dr. Charles Dodgson (1832 - 1898) was a mathematical lecturer at Oxford who also wrote nonsense poems and books to entertain children. He is best known for 'Alice in Wonderland' and 'Alice Through the Looking Glass' which he wrote to for Alice Liddell, daughter of the Dean of Christchurch.

And for **Professor Crystal** it is a simple leap from this sort of Victorian parlour game word-play to the cross-word puzzles, scrabble-games and even punning newspaper headlines of today. In this respect, he quotes with pleasure the headline that saluted the journey aboard the Space Shuttle at the age of 77 made by former pioneering astronaut, John Glenn:

'*To Oldly Go*' began the Independent's article. Now I had not intended to read that article, I was in a hurry that morning, but I just had to read it after seeing such a wonderful pun at the top. I read the article. And that was exactly what was in the copy writer's mind.

Peter Holland observes:

Language now is exploding at the same speed as it was exploding in the Renaissance. It's as if there has been a comparative lull across a couple of centuries and suddenly there's a new exhilaration in the way that language can be developed. But the new languages that we invent, the new words that we import into language, come from what are essentially jargons, sub-languages, the kind of scientific languages that get across into our speech. Thus, we all speak '*computerese*' now, so that the mouse is no longer simply a small furry animal, it now means for us something you push around with your hand while you're playing on the computer screen.

And with that language coming from, particularly, the sciences, it doesn't get infused with quite the same playfulness. There are a few exceptions, for instance, when a scientist was looking for a word that described a particular attribute of matter and picked up the word *quark* from James Joyce.

But **Professor Holland's** slightly pessimistic view of the language play involved in word-creation today is at variance with the experience of humorist, Steve Punt, who believes that the urge to use words imaginatively and invent new, albeit jokey, words to suit changing circumstances is as vigorous as ever:

I travel to town by train and within days of Railtrack replacing British Rail a few years ago, it was known to all commuters as 'Snailtrack'. The same thing happened with Network South East, it became known as 'NOTwork South East'.

Punt reckons that there is in fact more, not less, punning around in Britain at the start of the third millennium. He cites the press that has moved from rigorous formality at the beginning of the twentieth century to ubiquitous and often very inventive punning - David Crystal's 'To Oldly Go' is but one tiny example. Word play is ubiquitous. Few areas of human activity, except those where precision and absolutely scrupulous linguistic accuracy are essential, such as the law, are now immune to it.

Thus, many of the rules of appropriateness of language are being stretched, if not broken, to accommodate word play, because word play is attractive, dynamic, memorable. It calls upon powerful human emotions like humour; uses many of the tools of poetry - assonance, rhythm, rhyme etc.; and is widely and routinely employed commercially to promote, sell, persuade. It is perhaps the most powerful linguistic tool available to users of English today. So crucial is it, says **David Crystal**, it can control your destiny:

There's a great truth here, that people who really bond well together enjoy each other's language play - whatever it is, whether it's a pun, whether it's a funny tone of voice. And, when the day comes that somebody says 'I can't stand your silly voices' or 'why are you always making those stupid jokes', that's the day when the relationship is really not going to be a relationship for much longer. So language play, it seems to me, can be an immensely serious business at times.

Glossary

Various devices are used in word play. Some are well known poetic devices such as:

ALLITERATION

which occurs when several words which begin with the same letter are placed together in a sentence or phrase to gain a particular effect, as in: 'wild west wind' or, more elaborately in Tennyson's line: 'Portions and parcels of the dreadful past'. It is frequently used in advertising in order to make a product memorable. Sometimes it can be developed into a tongue twister such as 'She sells sea shells on the sea shore'.

ASSONANCE

is similar to alliteration. It is a form of internal rhyme when the resemblance of sound between two syllables in nearby words, arising from the rhyming of two or more accented vowels, is used for effect. Example: 'we were the first that ever burst into that silent sea'

HOMONYM

is a word with the same sound as another but a different meaning Example: you and yew. Similarly, a **HOMOPHONE** is a word which has the same sound as another but a different meaning, origin or spelling eg. pair, pear. **SYNONYM**, on the other hand, is a word which means the same or nearly the same as another in the same language. 'Close' and 'shut' are synonyms. English is full of them because it has taken words from so many different sources and there is often an overlap. These homonyms and synonyms provide the basis for many sorts of puns and types of word play.

Linguists use certain words to define their ideas. Common ones are:

ETYMOLOGY

meaning the sources of the formation of a word and the development of its meaning

MORPHOLOGY

which means the study of the forms of things. It might be the study of forms of words or the system of forms in a language or

NEOLOGISM

which means a new word or expression. The word can also be used to mean 'the coining of new words or expressions'. Very often people speak of a new 'coinage' which is a simple word for a neologism.

LEXIS

meaning words or vocabulary, and lexeme, meaning a word, also occurs in linguistics. They come from the same Greek word which has given us lexicographer, meaning a compiler of dictionaries or lexicon meaning vocabulary.

Some word play is based on mixing words up or transposing the sounds of different words:

MALAPROPISM

is the confusion of two words which sound familiar and are often used for comic effect. The word *malaprop* originates from the French mal à propos, meaning inappropriate or inopportune, but most people think of it in relation to Mrs Malaprop, a character in Richard Sheridan's play 'The Rivals' who constantly confuses words for comic effect. An example of a malapropism is to say 'she danced a flamingo' rather than a 'flamenco'.

SPOONERISM

is the transposition, usually by accident, of the initial letters of two or more words. This is named after the Rev W.A Spooner 1844-1930 who was an English scholar and Warden of New College, Oxford and much given to confusing words in this way. Some people are particularly prone to this habit and it has been suggested that they suffer from a mild disability similar to dyslexia. Many of Spooner's remarks are famous. In a sermon in New College Chapel he pronounced that 'our Lord is indeed a shoving leopard' and is rumoured to have upbraided an idle student by saying: 'Sir, you have tasted a whole worm. You have hissed my mystery lectures. You were fighting a liar in the quadrangle.You will leave Oxford by the town drain'. However, the fact that this must have been recounted by the student suggests that it is an inventive rather than reliable report.

A BETTER
CLASS OF
LANGUAGE

Class. The British disease. The British obsession. As a nation we seem to volley constantly between obsessive me-too-ism and stand-offish elitism. Still, in the Britain of New Labour, where the consensual politics of the 'Third Way' are supposed to draw us together, the barriers between classes are as robust as ever. It's just that the elites are differently constituted. The things that bond groups together are not so much common religious beliefs or political views, as perhaps they were in the past. What seems to bond people now is very often similarity of style, whether in choosing designer labels, or music to listen to, or simply where to go for entertainment. But what of language? Where does the way we speak fit into the evolving pattern of class in Britain?

In 1954, John Betjeman delivered a witty, stinging verse attack on the supposed inappropriateness of particular social manners and the vocabulary that goes, or did fifty years ago, with them. In a poem called 'How to Get on in Society' he made fun of the sort of middle class woman who uses the words 'serviettes' and 'cruets', who puts frills round the lamb cutlets and heats her house with an electric fire designed to look like a real fire with logs in the grate. It is a cruel and accurate satirical sketch of the sort of pretentious vocabulary often used by people who want to be posh, but betray their insecurity by unnecessary affectation. Betjeman disliked the usages he lampoons. 'Kiddies','dainty serviettes', 'toilets' and their 'requisites', not to mention the' cruet' on the table all take a tumble in the first two stanzas. In the rest of the poem, he has a go at the use of 'close' to mean humid, 'lounge' for drawing-room,'vestibule' for hall as well as other such well-known 'frowned-upons' as 'couch' (say sofa), 'sweet' (for dessert) and 'preserve' (instead of jam). What, though, is intrinsically wrong with these words? They are perfectly adequate as words. They do a perfectly functional job.They designate clearly and unambiguously the objects they describe. So what is all the fuss?

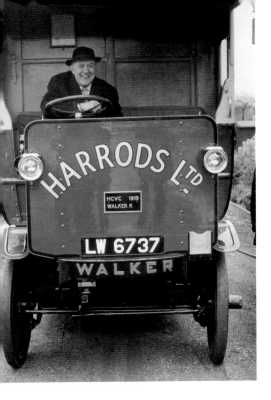

The fact is, of course, that language, all language, is more than merely functional. We 'read' words for their direct meaning, yet we also read them, continuously though often unconsciously, for their resonances. What sort of person is the speaker? Are they intelligent? Are they using a sophisticated or perhaps unusual vocabulary? Is she or he like me? Are we compatible? In 1956 Nancy Mitford edited a collection of essays in which were discussed U (Upper class) and non-U ways of speaking. The writers make clear the social dividing line between those who talked, for instance, about 'mantlepieces' rather than about 'chimney pieces', and about 'mirrors' rather than 'looking glasses'.

The idea that a person's class and place in society is defined by the way they speak, and particularly the way they sound their vowels, is a long standing snobbery in England. In George Bernard Shaw's play 'Pygmalion', the flower seller, Eliza Doolittle, attracts the attention of Professor Henry Higgins with her Cockney speech. He takes on a bet to completely change the way she speaks in such a way that everyone will be convinced she was born a member of the upper class. Higgins is middle class and Eliza is not and the way the two speak and behave to one another reveals what for several centuries have been the established prejudices about class and speech. Upper class people speak in a way which observes the grammatical rules of standard English and relates closely to written standard English. The uneducated working class speak in a more heavily

Non-standard accents may have been stigmatised but there was another side. Working men had their own vocabularies often originating from their trade. Miners talk, for example, of 'winning the coal', that is, getting the coal out of the seam. BBC radio producer, Charles Parker, introduced the voices, lives and concerns of ordinary working men and women in his moving documentaries in the 1950s and 1960s

accented way, using less regular grammar and pronouncing words in a more 'sloppy' manner, often running one syllable into another or slurring the vowel sounds. Although, in his play, Shaw is partly laughing at Professor Higgins for his obsession with language and class and his insensitivity to Eliza as a person, he is also pointing out the power of 'correct' pronunciation - described by linguists as 'Received Pronunciation'. Shaw may have set out to question whether Higgins is right to treat Eliza in this way, 'improving' her speech for his own satisfaction, but the rags-to-riches structure of the plot leaves the audience in no doubt that Eliza is better off when she can say 'hurricanes hardly happen' without dropping her 'hs' than when she relies on cockney insults for conversational effect. Ironically, we accept the rightness of the Henry Higginses of this world in their mission to 'improve' the speech of the working class.

Yet all is today not so straightforward. Sixty-five years ago, the writer, George Orwell, travelled to the industrial areas of the north of England. In his classic essay, 'The Road to Wigan Pier', he makes some pertinent observations about the people he met, and about attitudes to class. Orwell, a 'down at heel member of the bourgeoisie' as he calls himself, remembers class attitudes he encountered in his own family as a boy: the young Eric Blair (Orwell was a pseudonym) had played on building sites and had gone bird-nesting with the children of the local plumber '...*but it was not long before I was forbidden to play with the plumber's children; they were 'common' and I was told to keep away from them. This was snobbish,*' he writes, '*but it was also necessary, for middle-class people cannot allow their children to grow up with vulgar accents...*' Repeatedly, Orwell characterises the accepted view prevalent in his childhood that accent and class went hand in hand: '*Common people seemed almost sub-human. They had coarse faces, hideous accents and gross manners..*'

And though Orwell, as a fervent socialist, rejects the views he grew up with, and sympathises with the pitiable conditions in which the poor working people of northern England were surviving in 1937, he does lament the poverty of expression of one hopeless case who endlessly repeats *'It does seem 'ard, don't it now?* However, to be fair, in the same essay, he lambasts *'the poverty of the modern upper-class dialect'* with equal venom: *'the speech of 'educated' people is now so lifeless and characterless that a novelist can do nothing with it...'*

Of course, the world has turned many times since Orwell was able to publish these thoughts. In the world of politics, we have moved from the patrician tones of prime ministers like Harold Macmillan and Alec Douglas-Home, through the era of the Wilsonian northern resonance, the Callaghan rasp and - the new levelled out norm - the flat south-London vowels of the Major era. But, despite this apparent evolution and growing acceptance of non-posh speech in the highest office in government, throughout the past fifty years, grammatical infelicities, mispronunciations and, often as not, strong regional accents have continued to be sniggered at. Foreign Secretary, Ernest Bevin was laughed at in the late 1940s for calling clichés 'clitches' and the Deputy Prime Minister, John Prescott, is constantly lampooned for his tortuous grammar - or lack of it. The class connection with language never fails to be made.

So where did this seemingly indissoluble link between class and ways of speaking come from? Clearly it was a fact of life as far as Orwell and his parents were concerned at the start of the twentieth century. In reality the history of the social stigmatising of 'non-standard' accents and grammar goes back a lot further, at least two hundred or more years.

It is not a feature of language or society that can be dated exactly, but certainly the *idea* of an 'approved' way of speaking, and, by contrast, of a form which would invite criticism or even social ostracism, is linked very closely to the expansion of interest in, and attention to, language and its regularisation. This has its roots in the sixteenth and seventeenth centuries, but comes to prominence in the eighteenth, at just the same moment as the Industrial Revolution is shifting the balance of urban and agricultural populations and beginning to allow new social mobility.

There is always a lot of discussion about whether regional accents were frowned on prior to the eighteenth century in the way they were later. Experts in language often disagree about this. In the first *Routes of English* book, **Martin Starkie**, Director of the Geoffrey Chaucer Centre in Canterbury, made the point that in 'The Canterbury Tales', the speech of Aleyn and John, the students of the 'Reeve's Tale', is written in a dialect which is clearly from the north of England, and at that time was considered by those in the south of the country as barbarous. However, **Lynda Mugglestone** of Pembroke College, Oxford, presents a different view. She points out that Aleyn and John are far from being northern nitwits;

> They are the 'educated' and 'superior' characters'; it is the Miller who is of lower
> status, and a loser, too.

So, a regional flavour to one's speech, while marking someone out as different, maybe even as a target for mockery, is not a clear indicator that they are not 'one of us'. In fact, the 'aspirational' language of medieval England would not have been 'posh English' at all, but the courtly language of the monarchs and their entourage, namely French.

As **Dr. Kathryn Lowe** of Glasgow University observes:

Isaac Newton, for example, who was actually very interested in phonetics and

pronunciation, in his writings tries out a little bit of basic phonetics. And from that we can tell that he had a very, very strong Lincolnshire accent. This is hard to imagine in a way, because you always think of these people as sort of posh grandees. But they often had strong accents.

So, for the big leap to really 'classy' talk, you have to wait until one sort of English can be said to exist, a standard form of expression that will serve as a reference point for the whole country. In the early Middle Ages, there was no such language as standard English. In the year 1000, all English, essentially, was regional, and though there were large groupings of broadly similar speech, there was no spoken standard.

The advent of printing in the fifteenth century, and with it, the ability to make repeated identical copies of the same text, began to establish the notion of conformity. Copies did now conform, at least amongst themselves, so a degree of standardisation began to appear in English. However, English was still thoroughly regional, and though the capital and its talk obviously exerted a powerful influence, there was still not in Shakespeare's day a national norm. Shakespeare himself is thought to have spoken with a broad Warwickshire accent.

Social snobbery is as old as society itself and one has only to think of the affectations of some of Shakespeare's more eccentric courtiers to see that certain sorts of behaviour have been ridiculed since the dawn of civilisation. For example, in 'Hamlet' Osric, the courtier, speaks in terms of excessive flattery about Laertes:

'Believe me, an absolute gentleman, full of most excellent differences, of very soft society, and great showing: indeed, to speak feelingly of him, he is the card and calendar of gentry, for you shall find in him the continent of what part a gentleman should be.'

There have always been the elect and the rest, the belongers and the outsiders, cabals and refusés.

The French playwright, Molière, lampoons the vain and the affected, and again Shakespeare takes a trowel to dunces and the lower orders. **Professor Peter Holland** of Birmingham University who runs the Shakespeare Centre at Stratford makes the point that the drunken Porter in 'Macbeth' is a piece of Elizabethan stand-up comedy. His repeated: *'Knock, knock, knock! Who's there I' the name of Beelzebub'* provides a good example of the Elizabethan lower orders as does Fluellen in 'Henry V. However, it is mainly for his Welshness that Fluellen is ridiculed rather than for his accent. **Dr. Kathryn Lowe** comments:

I'm particularly interested in the way in which people start to stigmatise non-standard accents. Richard Mulcaster, who was Headmaster of Merchant Taylor's School in London in the sixteenth century (and was, incidentally, very interested in spelling reform), spoke with a strong northern accent. And apparently the Inspectors complained to Richard Mulcaster that the children weren't being taught to pronounce their vowels properly because there were so many Northerners there!

That's very interesting because we haven't really seen that happening before. We've seen the stigmatisation of *written* English, but not *spoken* English, and this is going to become more and more apparent.

People are going to want to speak properly, and we're going to see in the seventeenth and eighteenth centuries a number of grammars coming into play which try to teach people to use grammar correctly.

Dr. Lowe singles out, as a landmark in this process, a book written in 1589 by George

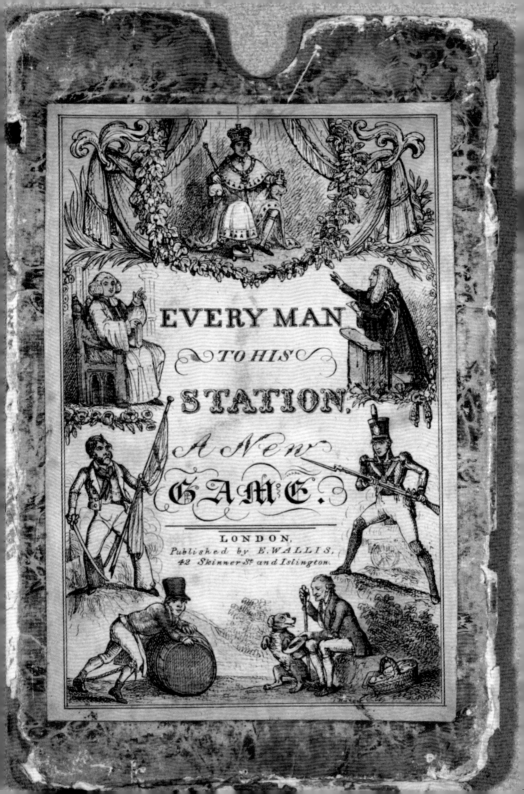

EVERY MAN

TO HIS

STATION,

A New

GAME.

LONDON.
Published by E. WALLIS,
42 Skinner St and Islington.

Even Victorian board games, such as this one, show a preoccupation with definitions of class. Instead of concentrating on buying Park Lane, as Monopoly does, the Victorians saw achievement as rising from one class to another.

Puttenham entitled 'The Arte of English Poesie' in which he spells out the most appropriate form of language for budding poets:

He says you shouldn't really be using anything from the North; no use looking to Langland, no use looking to Gower. Very interestingly, no use looking back at Chaucer, because we don't understand him. What we really ought to be taking is the speech of London, he said, *'but not of carters, because they mangle their vowels'*. Isn't that interesting - they mangle their vowels! Poets should aim for the better brought-up sort of speech, he says. So basically he's advocating the use of speech within London, or about sixty miles around.

Changes to the status of English vis-à-vis Latin, and the latter's decline as the preferred language of scholarship in favour of the vernacular, helped push English centre-stage. By the early eighteenth century (in 1712) Jonathan Swift, the literary genius and satirist who wrote 'Gulliver's Travels' was proposing an Academy to oversee the regulation of English. A year earlier, the essayist Joseph Addison had recommended the establishment of what he called 'Superintendents' who would act as custodians of the language. Their concern was with good grammar, yet there were already well-established commentaries on the sounds of English.

One of the first public legislators of the language and arbiter of 'good' and 'bad' English was, as **Lynda Mugglestone** points out in her book on class and the English language, another eighteenth century writer, Thomas Sheridan. Sheridan gave a series of popular public lectures at Oxford and published several language guides, one of which (an account of his *Course of Lectures*) condemns *'the false pronunciation of certain words peculiar to each county. Surely'*, continues Sheridan, *'every gentleman will think it worthwhile to take some pains, to get rid of such evident marks of rusticity....'*

This little self-help manual, 'Poor Letter H - its use and abuse' is thought to have been written by 'The Hon. Henry H.' This cartoon on the front depicts an Alice-in-Wonderland-Red-Queen-like dowager bearing aloft a parasol and on her face an expression of extreme hauteur. Doffing his top hat is a gentleman of quality. So dropping 'Hs' was not just a failing of the lower classes.

Prescription was the order of the age. It is the term used by linguists to describe the laying down of cast-iron rules about the grammar and pronunciation of English. This was the first great flourishing of the dictionary-makers and the notion of prescription flourished with them. Dr. Johnson's Dictionary of 1755 set the standard of the age for English and was hailed as a triumph for the nation. Now notions of 'correctness' and 'good English' are yoked to ideas of refinement and breeding. One has only to look at the actual vocabulary that is deployed to detect the fatal attraction of linguistic and social correctness. Thus *vulgarity, rudeness, ugliness, plebeian, parvenu, Cockney, barbarism, slovenly, uneducated, embarrassing* and *ridiculous* are spoken in the same breath, while their 'positive' counterparts easily find themselves jogging along together: *purity of accent, educated, cultivated, polish, lady, gentleman* and *refinement.* The message is quite clear: good standard English, well-spoken, is the indicator of good breeding and high-class. John Walker's 'Critical Pronouncing Dictionary' of 1791 made him an icon of the age, such that he came to bear the soubriquet 'Elocution' Walker.

Now as we move into the Victorian era, the class issue becomes even more sharply defined. 'How To Get On In Society' was a publication from 1860 devoted to social advancement which stated: *'Purity of accent is the grand distinctive feature of an educated gentleman...'*

This was the era of Disraeli's Two Nations: the great masses of urban poor who kept the wheels of the Industrial Revolution turning and the wealthy classes who enjoyed a life of leisure. The poor spoke roughly whereas the others spoke in a way they considered refined. Even the manufacturers, the great self-made factory bosses whose enterprise steered the industrial expansion, were not immune to the sneering of the prescriptivists

"Please, Ma'am, you've dropped something."

for being rough and ready in their speech.

By the middle of the nineteenth century, the self-help manuals, bent on turning readers' common speech into genteel discourse, were becoming a huge growth industry. And it was the dropping of aitches, and the 'h' application to words where they 'ave no place that above all seemed to consume the Victorian language deans. One particular hit was a sixpenny guide called 'Poor Letter H - Its Use and Abuse' which ran to forty editions.

But 'Poor Letter H' was far from alone and lost; 'Harry Hawkins' H Book' and 'Mind Your Hs' went hand in hand with 'Mind Your Hs and Take Care of Your Rs' and 'Common Blunders in Speaking and How to Avoid Them.' It was a battleground out there, so much so that Henry Sweet (an authority on Anglo-Saxon and the history of the English language and, incidentally, the model for Professor Higgins in 'Pygmalion') writing in 1890 could say of the poor letter 'H' that its observance was *an almost infallible test of education and refinement'*.

It is thus not surprising that George Orwell, born just over a decade later, found himself in a world where 'speaking proper' was a passport to gentility and where a slough of dropped aitches, inserted redundant 'r's and omitted final 'ng's was a desperate fate to be avoided like a communicable disease.

Richard Hoggart is the author of 'The Uses of Literacy', a seminal work about language and the way it works in British society, that has dominated thinking for forty years or more. He remembers the tug of language at home in Yorkshire as a boy, when 'talking

71

proper' was what you did in public; at home you could speak broad. It is a practice that linguists refer to as 'code-switching':

At home I just spoke Yorkshire. But when I got to school it was a sort of educated Yorkshire put on for the masters. The English master would have chased me round the room if I had spoken broad.

And you went all the way down, until you got to the real basic working class, and we had no difficulty at all in recognising them. They were the ones who, even now if you go past a building site, can't complete a sentence or even sometimes a clause without saying 'f*' - and you wonder why they have to say it so often. It's f***ing this, f***ing that.**

And yet and yet... The world was undoubtedly on the turn. Though the star-crossed lovers of mid-century masterpieces like the film 'Brief Encounter' still declared their hopeless passion in the pinched vowels and crystalline consonants of what linguists call 'Advanced Received Pronunciation', the world knew that this was not how they really spoke. At the same time, ordinary folk's speech with its rougher realities of imperfect enunciation was beginning to be heard. The great film documentarists of the 1930s, like John Grierson, had begun to celebrate the honest toil of the ordinary workman and Orwell's 'Road to Wigan Pier', though aware of perceptions about infra-dig accents, nonetheless championed the lives of the working poor.

BBC Radio has had an important role in exemplifying the way people speak. In the past it has been largely responsible for defining what is now regarded as standard spoken English. Announcers, commentators, news readers have spoken with the same basically London accent and this has come to be accepted as 'Received Pronunciation'. At the same time, it has ushered sounds from everywhere into every home which has a radio

and begun to allow the accented voices of everyman on to the air. The lives and raw, ordinary voices of men and women doing hard jobs on the railways, in trawlers and underground in the mines have been presented in documentary programmes. Charles Parker, a well known radio producer in the 1950s and 1960s, put these richly savourable accents and moving articulacy centre-stage. They were no longer the 'samples' and 'examples' to be gazed at down the social historian's microscope. These were men and women who could speak movingly and graphically about their lives and their labour, words which Parker crafted into broadcast eloquence.

Today, 'Advanced Received Pronunciation' is broadly seen as undesirable, and amongst many young people it is a social handicap. It has to be dulled and 'roughed up' into something approaching the relatively class-less speech of John Major and so-called 'Estuary English'.

So, who speaks what, today? And what conclusions can we draw about the snobbery, or at least the class-consciousness, of how people speak in Britain at the beginning of the twenty-first century? The snobbery certainly still has a powerful influence. **Richard Hoggart** commenting on the language of class, talked about his own roots in working class Leeds:

I think it doesn't lead you very far just to talk about 'the working classes' as though they are or were one. They weren't in our day. We knew them intimately; we were the respectable working class. We spoke Yorkshire, but could be terribly genteel, like my aunt, for example. She had a real 'Marshall & Snelgrove' voice. She was very uneasy, but she had it superimposed on a Yorkshire voice.

People will always want to improve themselves and, perhaps, to give the impression that they are more refined than they really are. At the same time, people who pride themselves on being upper class will always think up ways of shoring up their sense of being an elite by erecting barriers against intruders into that elite. They will set up private languages or slang expressions which, to begin with, are meaningless to others. But the world has changed a lot in the last fifty years and communication is now both faster and more pervasive. The media seeks out and exposes every aspect of style, particularly different language styles. Fashions in expression, as in everything else, change increasingly swiftly and fame and fortune depend on catching those fashions. It is no longer necessary to speak with a certain sort of accent to become successful and wealthy, nor does a broad accent of any sort debar people from becoming glamorous and famous. Energy and self confidence are now as important as a knowledge of what is correct. Style is everything. Life is fuller and faster and spoken English gains from the variety this brings.

4

UNSPEAKABLE ENGLISH

'I swear by Almighty God to tell the truth, the whole truth and nothing but the truth...' This is the oath of honesty given before every court of law, and the primary definition of 'to swear' in the dictionary is '*to make a solemn declaration or statement with an appeal to God*'. *Swerian* is a good old-fashioned Anglo-Saxon word, from the Germanic verb *swarjan*. But where does swearing come from, and oaths for that matter? The bad words, the 'unspeakable' English that is this chapter's heading?

The concept of swearing goes deep into the heart of our society - to our belief in God, to notions of loyalty and obedience given on oath, to ordered social systems that depend on allegiance that is absolute and sworn. Up-ending that allegiance, displacing that order, breaking that loyalty or even taking religious beliefs in vain represent the disordering of society. Swearing, then, in the sense of speaking profanely, flies in the face of accepted order. 'Taking the name of the Lord in vain' is a way of upsetting accepted values and rebelling against the authority which enables a secure society to be established on those values. Similarly, the other sort of swearing, which is based on sexual innuendo or crude reference to bodily functions, is a rebellion against politeness, against the dignity of human life and against 'accepted' behaviour. Another way of rebelling against that society is to upturn the rules of politeness. Coarse references to sex or unmentionable bodily functions is another way of swearing. It is not profanity against God, but rebellion against the conventions which used to be so important to a stable society. DH Lawrence's novel 'Lady Chatterley's Lover' was censored because it contained obscene words and might subvert social values. A long debate took place in court as to whether the book's literary merits outweighed its obscenity.

Nowadays on a busy commuter train anywhere in Britain you are likely to hear someone mouthing off to someone else, maybe yelling into a mobile phone, about how *bloody* late

the train is running or what a *f***ing* awful day they have had. The allegiance stuff seems pretty far away now. Yet the sense of disorder, of upsetting the norms of polite behaviour is still the impetus behind the energy people put into using foul language. Think of a time when you have been tempted to earwig someone who's been spilling profanities across a street or perhaps aimed a mouthful at you through an open car window. Did you feel aggressed? Did you feel upset? Maybe not. But there was probably sufficient verbal energy knocking about to upset some more sensitive souls. That is the reason why swearing on radio and television have such a profound effect, still, on the audience. Swear-words are *energetic* bits of language. They are designed to shock the hearer to attack him or her perhaps, and correspondingly to ease frustration and tension on the part of the utterer. Swearing is a verbal thunderstorm: there is lots of letting off of energy and occasionally some damage caused.

A thousand years ago, though, in the first couple of centuries of the English language, swearing meant, as we have seen from the dictionary definition, the uttering of a solemn declaration, with an appeal to the deity. **Geoffrey Hughes**, formerly Professor of English at the University of Witwatersrand and author of one of the most authoritative histories of swearing, traces the development from formal oath-**taking** to informal oath-**uttering** thus:

In the Middle Ages, of course, people swore 'on the Bible', 'by their mother's grave' or something like that, by some higher force, with astonishing profusion. Then they 'swore to do' something, what we now perhaps call 'an oath of heroic or serious undertaking'. That subsequently evolved into swearing at people, then just swearing to let off steam. As you can see, you're moving down the social scale from the Almighty to an area which was well defined by the writer, Ian Fleming, as 'midway between the solar plexus and the upper thigh.'

But if solemn swearing was a common practice in medieval Britain, what curses or profanities did the Anglo-Saxons fill their mouths with, or was this form of expression not part of their culture or language? The answer is difficult to determine with any certainty since, as we have often admitted during these *Routes of English* enquiries, we clearly have very little evidence of true spoken English from the early years of the second millennium. This is no more true than of so-called bad language, which is a quintessential part of spoken English and which is so often, even today, modified, softened or ignored in written texts. A particular problem, when it comes to Anglo-Saxon literature is that, according to **Geoffrey Hughes**:

We don't really have any Anglo-Saxon street-talk. The literature which has survived is of a generally very high moral tone. What we do see, though, is a very clear cultural emphasis on what you might call 'verbal responsibility'. That's to say that language should be used in a way which must be respected, and not in a loose way. There are instances in the Anglo-

Saxon laws that state that people should not 'swear by the pagan gods', which would probably indicate that they did. There is also in the literature an emphasis on reticence: one should not say anything which might lead to a confrontation.

And **Dr. Kathryn Lowe** of Glasgow University, who is an expert in the Old English spoken by our Anglo-Saxon forebears, agrees with Professor Hughes that the religious tenor of the Old English texts that have come down to us presents problems when trying to get to grips with street-talk:

If you take a good, old-fashioned battle, like the battle of Maldon of 991, I'm sure that people were coming out with all sorts of rude words, but the only thing that seems to have survived is a thing which is described as a 'curse', which is *abreode his angin*, and it means 'may his enterprise fail'. This is what a man says after somebody has deserted and essentially lost the battle. But I don't honestly think that they would have come up with something quite as nice as that: I'm sure they would have had rather more suitable epithets for that man!

It seems likely that the Anglo-Saxons were probably as profane as any of the succeeding users of the English language.

Let us tackle the question from the other end, as it were. It is, of course, one of the clichés of modern euphemism to refer generically to swear words as 'Anglo-Saxonisms'. Because that is where they originated, presumably. **Dr. Lowe** ran through a short checklist of the standard so-called Anglo-Saxonisms and begs to differ:

I'm sorry to have to disappoint you, but very few of our popular swear words are actually Old English in origin. In fact, the origin of some of them is shrouded in mystery. If you take the 'f' word for example, that's actually first recorded in the sixteenth century. There's a German

More marital upset, with a wife brandishing a weapon from her domestic work: a wooden skimmington ladle. Glimpses into the actual words uttered in conflicts in and out of the home are given in court records. One such is recorded in Whitechapel in 1610 when Alice Rochester insulted Jane Lilham on a doorstep in front of their neighbours with these words: 'Thou art a whore and an arrant whore and a common carted whore'...Words mattered and sexual slander was not always a joking matter for 6 months later Jane sued Alice for slander.Hundreds of other women did so every year, and their words are a great source for the historian of language and its social context.

verb *ficken*, which obviously means the same thing. However, the two can't actually be shown to be related. So that one's a problem.

The '*c*' word is also not recorded in Old English and isn't found before the thirteenth century (after the Anglo-Saxon period), although there are related words in other Germanic languages.

The word 'shit' is Old English,but it's not common and it just seems to refer to diarrhoea, and a similar rather unfortunate malady concerning cattle as well. Incidentally, the Anglo-Saxons had other words for diarrhoea. For example, there's a wonderful, if rather unpleasant adjective, *utirnende* - which meant literally 'running out'!

If you take another staple of our swearing wordhoard, 'bugger', that isn't Old English either. It's actually derived from the Latin *bulgarus* and first appears in the fourteenth century.'Bugger' is very interesting because the Latin *bulgarus* just refers to a sect of heretics that came to Bulgaria in the eleventh century and originally it has that meaning of 'heretic'. The reason it attains the meaning it has today is because heretics were apparently well known for getting up to all sorts of dodgy practices, hence 'sodomite'.

The essayist, William Hazlitt, writing at the end of the eighteenth century, declared that the English were '*a rather foul-mouthed nation*'. To what extent this is true is difficult to judge - every nation utters oaths, profanities and curses at some time and in considerable volume at certain times. What is certainly true is that, during the Middle Ages at the time of Joan of Arc and the wars between France and England, the French knew the British, or at least the English, as *Les Godemmes*. This was an approximation in French of the English oath 'God-damn' and they earned this soubriquet, allegedly, because 'God-damn' was the term most associated with them at that time.

Rife you drunken Slaue.

But, if the large rich and colourful stock of unspeakable English that has come down to us today is not strictly of Anglo-Saxon origin, it certainly begins to show itself in great abundance by the time Geoffrey Chaucer was setting down his 'Canterbury Tales' in the last years of the fourteenth century. **Professor Geoffrey Hughes** savours some of the most interesting:

We see a wonderful profusion of oaths, extraordinary ones, in this wonderful cavalcade of 'The Canterbury Tales' by Chaucer, some of which really make our hair stand on end now, mainly to do with the agony and suffering of the Crucifixion. In the 'Pardoner's Tale' Chaucer writes: *'and many a grisly ooth thanne han they sworn. And Cristes blessed body al torente'* **which was really sort of 'tore apart', and you get** *'Goddes precious herte'*, *'Benedicite'*, **which is from St Benedict,** *'Goddes digne bones'*, **meaning 'God's worthy bones'. Then again there's** *'Goddes armes'*, **and so on.**

Some are not simply profanities but curses, carrying a serious threat with them: *'Jhesu shorte thy lyf!'*, **in other words, 'may Jesus terminate you or** *'The feend ... yow fecche, body and bones'* **,in other words, 'the Devil take you, lock, stock and barrel'.**

At the same time you're getting the introduction of swearing which we understand or recognise more easily. When Chaucer's Wife of Bath refers to Metellius, a classical figure

A page from the Court Minute Books of the Governors of Bridewell and Bethlem, 1576. A woman called Thomasen Breame is being examined in the hospital court as to whether or not she earnt her living from prostitution.

The examination here is as it was written down by the court recorder in a sixteenth century script known as 'secretary hand'. The names in the left hand column (Deprosper, Shawe, Brownynge, Grene, Wise, Lodge) refer to people that Thomasen accuses of prostitution or bawdry (that is, running a brothel or procuring prostitutes.) In line 19 Thomasen claims that Mrs.Stalle was 'fulle of the poxe and a naughty pack'. 'Pack' meant a person of low or worthless character. 'Naughty' has subsequently lost its force and is not used now to describe adults in this context. Elsewhere in these records the court recorder uses Latin or latinate vocabulary such as 'carnal copulation' to refer to sexual intercourse rather than write down the actual taboo words that the examinants used.

'*as a foule cherl, the swyn*', that's the beginning of vituperation. I suppose. So the '*foul swin*' is perhaps the first instance of 'swine' used in the way that we would recognise it as a swear word.

The use of raw language describing bodily parts and functions as more than just that, that is, as foul-mouthed descriptions applied to people, seems to date from long after they first become current. **Dr. Kathryn Lowe** says:

Eventually they undergo some sort of pejoration and start to be applied to perhaps a specific person. Again, if you take a word like 'shit', you're not actually going to find that being applied to a man before the sixteenth century, and it doesn't really have popular use until the eighteenth, nineteenth century.

Though, in this case, **Geoffrey Hughes** observes that the compound *shit-breech* is found as a piece of abuse as early as 1202.

But in *The Routes of English,* what we are looking for is some record of the way the language actually worked in the mouths of our forebears. What did swearing actually sound like? How did people actually use these expressions? If it is difficult to uncover direct examples of the sound of medieval speech, it becomes easier as we come closer to modern times, as the records of the way people spoke (as opposed to *literary* versions of it) become more plentiful.

The records of words spoken in courts of law are an invaluable source of almost verbatim transcriptions of the speech of ordinary witnesses and defendants. The church of St Mary le Bow in Cheapside, London was, five hundred years ago, one of the places where church courts met. It was there, in the arched crypt, that **Dr. Laura Wright**, lecturer in English Language at the University of Cambridge and **Justin Champion**, history lecturer at

She saith that Emme Dep[...]ter the Italian doth Elizabeth Coroy and paid hd as well for it And [...] of [...] would come her to m[...] Procter and lete hir ther all night And yet she saith Also she saith that many [...] resorte to [...] And ther came company appoynted [...] And she saith marget Goldsmyth did know Emm D[...] at his owne house by [...]

The saith also that John Ch[...] and his wiffe dwelling nyer S Lawrence [...] many prentices and servante and [...] it is seid And that they lyve of no oder thinge but bawdrey and [...]

The saith also that marget Goldsmyth lyeth at one Brownynge howse in Colborne where Brownynge is a bande And he brought my [...] to be forget hir to me and to m[...] B[...]ge And from thenske they went to one Stalles house at wolfstakel hall And ther m[...] Stalle being full of the p[...] and a [...] park And ther they seid one Christian Breme a [...] sister of Whitefrier and they sleped ther togither One of the yonge men [...] on the muche [...] a fat fellow not hyghe She saith that m[...] Tomas lyeth at Brownynge

Also she sayd Thomasyn Breme saith that [...] wiffe tolde her of a propper compa[...] man with a little [...] hede very little or none [...] said [...] was very liberall and full of money And she said her [...] m[...] an alderman and one of the [...] m[...] in London [...] the lady Lap[...]

Also she thynketh that m[...] Lodge in Chester lane is [...] nought and [...] and [...] Em[...]

Royal Holloway College in London, met to discuss the oaths and language of common criminals as recorded in documents of the time. **Justin Champion**:

Church courts, like this one we're standing in, have become tremendously useful for historians in recent years, because they're one of the few sources that allow us to reconstruct ordinary everyday language. Church courts, both here and in the provinces, were spaces where both an ecclesiastical hierarchy and also the neighbourly community could try out their insults and prosecute each other for defamation, slander and libel.

There are some reservations. Obviously the language is mediated by literate officials, praetors, and a whole sort of network of ecclesiastical officials who used standard discourse, perhaps to translate some of their language. But certainly, in the case of women, the local community and neighbours, they would all actually invigorate the court process...There's a very famous example in the 1630s in Dorchester. Henry Gollop, the 'champion swearer' was recorded swearing forty times in one evening by a church warden who poked his nose through the keyhole. Sadly, when he was actually prosecuted, he managed another ten swear words.

It is naturally always open to question as to what extent these records can be taken as verbatim accounts of the way ordinary people spoke: the record is written down by a recorder who may have cleaned up the language for posterity. Even 'Hansard', the verbatim account of parliamentary proceedings, although complete and unabridged, is not the record of every cough, splutter, 'um' and 'er', and the text is tidied up for publication. There may also have been other reasons, to do with religious sensibilities, or simply the sorts of things that one would or would not utter in the formal surroundings of a courtroom, that may have led to abridgement or editing of the words spoken. However, these caveats are insignificant compared with the invaluable whiff of real life that blows through the transcripts from these court proceedings. **Dr. Laura Wright:**

It's never the case that any court recorder anywhere tends to write down all the 'um's and the 'ah's, the coughs and the cackles. What I would say is that when one is looking at church court records or hospital court records, or any kind of records where somebody was speaking aloud, and somebody then took down what they said, there are certain linguistic things that you can look out for: the way personal pronouns and names are used, for example. If they start to bundle together and to cluster together then you can be fairly sure that what you're getting is an attempt to write down what somebody said - as close to verbatim speech as we're ever going to get.

It was also significant in a court of law that the differences between the statements of different witnesses and the defendant were very exactly recorded, even if the meaning was very similar. It was the precise wording that was interesting to the court, so there you can be fairly sure of the accuracy as well.

Elizabethan swearing is rich in colour, witness hundreds, thousands, of examples in the bawdier bits of Shakespeare. The great collector of linguistic curiosities, Eric Partridge, published a whole, fascinating volume devoted to *Shakespeare's Bawdy*. Many of these today have lost their force, the unspoken social context being all-important to appreciating their full force. Yet they remain thoroughly recognisable in their invective style and by the sorts of bodily functions that crop up time and again. **Laura Wright** offers this mild example:

Let me tell you about a case on the 29th of August in 1561 that was brought before the Bridewell Hospital Court in London. A man called John Ashbury was brought into the court

'*for that he ys a Dronken quarrellinge knave and a rayller and a distruber of his neybors and a thrower of pispottes and bowles of pisse on their hedes and into their windowes and therfore was here well whipped the same daye and discharged.*' Those particular terms *a 'Dronken quarrellinge knave'*, '*a thrower of pispottes*' are perfectly recognisable. However, there are plenty in the church court records that are less clear to us.

One Mr Phipps is recorded as saying: '*I have found him that made the libell...that burnt pintle knave Rainulffe Mr Doylyes man*'. Nobody, so far as I know, goes around calling somebody else a '*burnt pintle knave*', and it's only by researching other contemporaneous documents that we know that '*burnt*' actually meant to convey 'suffering from a sexually-transmitted disease'. '*Pintle*' (meaning 'a penis') is a word that's still used dialectally in a very limited context with regard to animals.

Given a bit of careful research, you can begin to feel at least a little of the force of the insult, albeit in a rather academic way. Sadly for us, rather like explaining a joke, this process of decoding old oaths takes much of the force out of the lightning-strike that is their principal power. Other examples need a social context to help us understand them, as well as the linguistic codebook. **Laura Wright** quotes a church court case from Oxfordshire in 1610, in which a man speaking to a woman is recorded as declaring:

'*I can beget a boy, but Tull (the woman's husband) can beget nothing but squirt-tailed wenches*'. Now, on the face of it, that's not a particularly pleasant thing to say, but neither does it seem to be particularly evil or horrendous. But, when one starts to unpack what the phrase '*squirt-tailed wenches*' meant, I suspect it was far more potent then than we would recognise today.

This woodcut shows an early modern street scene: men working in the street, animals foraging for food, children playing outside. Two women are standing near their doorsteps, with one brandishing a staff at a man wearing cuckold's horns and a second emptying a chamber pot out of the window. Doorways and windows were important places in women's social and cultural life, for exchanging recipes and advice.

The reference to being only able to sire girls was already in Elizabethan England quite an insult. Add to that the expression *'squirt-tailed'*, which meant to have diarrhoea, and one begins to feel the way the language is leading. Add into the equation a social and health context in which diarrhoea was a common killer and the fact that this woman may already have had daughters who had died from diarrhoea and the expression becomes, what Dr. Wright calls, *'a horrendous thing to say, a horrible insult, whether it's true or not'*. Thus, as far as the history of bad language is concerned, context is indeed all.

If swearing is the aggressive utterance of the instant, the abusive equivalent of the witty rejoinder, it is little surprise that an evolving world of words should continually leave the abuse tagging along behind until it falls out of use altogether. It is not very different from that curious phenomenon, the nineteenth-century Punch cartoon that no longer has any humour left in it. It seems an eternal truth, therefore, as far as swearing is concerned, that *'age shall wither them'*. Most people can offer evidence from the past few years of the waning power of once unspeakable language. Eliza Doolittle's famous *'Not bloody likely'* in George Bernard Shaw's play 'Pygmalion' caused a furore when first uttered on the London stage. Yet today it sounds not even faintly quaint, so far did standards shift in the course of the twentieth century. **Justin Champion** quotes some now faded examples of abuse with religious connotations from far earlier:

If we look at the sort of commonplace blasphemy that gets into the church courts, we actually have a language that's almost emptied of any sort of violent meaning for us. If you call somebody an 'enthusiast' in the 1640s and 1650s, you're implying they're a 'ranter', they're inverting the social order, they're seditious, a threat to all sorts of hierarchy. The same was true of a 'fanatic', or a 'prophet', a 'tantivy'. These are all sort of rather quaint words, but in the Early Modern period (the Renaissance) they were powerful words of

abuse. Likewise *'God's wounds'*, *'God's blood'*, *'in the name of Christ'*, *'a pox on God'*. Today this is all pretty gentle stuff because we're not immersed in that religiously charged environment, where describing or using the wrong sort of language about Christ, about the Trinity, about the cleric, about the Church, is transgressive. We have to use an enormous amount of imagination, I think, to recreate that.

In his discussion with Professor Geoffrey Hughes and Dr. Kathryn Lowe, **Melvyn Bragg** picked up this point by quoting a fascinating verse, dating from the same period. It is an epigram written by Sir John Harrington, published in 1615:

In elder times an ancient custom was
To sweare in weighty matters by the Masse.
But when the Masse went down,(as old men note)
They sware then by the crossse of this same grote
And when the Crosse was likewise held in scorne,
Then by their faith, the common oath was sworne.
Last, having sworne away all faith and troth,
Only God damn them is their common oath.
Thus custome kept decorum by gradation,
That losing Masse, Crosse, Faith, they find damnation.

Sometimes, though, the dilution is deliberate and designed to make the unspeakable speakable. So 'bloody', which came from underworld slang about three hundred years ago, immediately spawned 'ruddy', 'blooming', 'bleeding', and 'b' as in 'the b. thing's broken'. Similarly, the 'f' word has spawned a wealth of euphemisms. From the eighteenth century, **Geoffrey Hughes** listed 'frigging' and 'footering' and from the twentieth

century 'footling' and, from about 1929, 'f***'.

These other forms spring up in the hinterland so to speak. And quite often, of course, people are not aware of their origins at all. For example,the word 'gor blimey' is a speakable form of 'God blind me'. And then people split the words up and say 'gor', or just 'cor', or 'blimey'.

As **Melvyn Bragg** pointed out, rhyming slang is often used to disguise an obscenity. Thus 'Hampton Wick' is rhyming slang for 'prick' and the word 'wick' which sounds harmless enough can be commonly used in place of 'prick':

Although, when we say 'to dip one's wick', there's still a slight embarrassment around. Lots and lots of people say 'he gets on my wick', 'they get on my wick', in front of the children, as it were.

But if swear words can hide behind euphemisms or such 'displaced' formulations as rhyming slang equivalents (that end up being freely used without embarrassment), being 'unspeakable' they are also often subject to censorship and excision. **Kathryn Lowe:**

In Elizabethan times playwrights tried to get round this by introducing words which were obviously intended to be the original word, but were in some way circumnavigated. But, the censors were on to that as well and they soon cut out those words, so it's been a continual line of progress, if you like.

And **Geoffrey Hughes** quotes two fascinating examples of this sort of censorship at work:

There was a sudden emergence in the eighteenth century of the word 'donkey', because

'ass' had developed an uncomfortable phonetic proximity to 'arse', and likewise 'rabbit' emerging because 'cony', pronounced 'cunny', was getting very close to the 'c' word.

As we have seen on a number of occasions during these *Routes of English* enquiries , the advent of broadcasting in the twentieth century has made a significant impact on the way language has developed. Since the creation of the first radio station in Britain, the British Broadcasting Company, in 1923, bad language has been subject to intense scrutiny by broadcasters and by the public. The Corporation's first Director-General, Sir John Reith, was an austere man with very strict morals and conduct who made absolutely certain that no language of a suggestive, improper or vulgar nature was broadcast.

When the critic, Kenneth Tynan, uttered the word the 'f' word on live TV in 1965, it caused a national scandal, though many saw it as a breakthrough moment for broadcasting. It came at a time when social attitudes towards sex, relationships and male and female roles were evolving very rapidly. That English, as it was heard on the air, should reflect these changes was not surprising. The shock, however, of the 'unutterable' word being spoken in normal conversation, available to all types and ages via television, was palpable.

Today, BBC Radio and Television still maintain very strict control over what bad language is permitted to be aired at what time. On television, the so-called 'watershed' of nine o'clock in the evening acts as a divide between restricted and stronger material, in terms of violence and sexual content in behaviour and language. But these days, after the watershed, dramas and films containing the full range of contemporary swear words are permissible, although they are subject to control and films are still 'edited for bad language'. These are, however, usually transmitted with what is known as a 'health warning' that refers to strong language.

On radio, where no such watershed exists, strong language is subject to considerable scrutiny and several of the terms, currently judged most offensive, are subject to referral to authority. This difference is partly the result of the way in which viewers and listeners perceive bad language. Radio has an intimacy (and is used with an intimacy) that television rarely attains. In addition, the addition of picture changes the perception of the swear words uttered. On radio, they remain bald and unadorned, and continue to possess the power to shock of the bolt of lightning.

Melvyn Bragg, who has worked in broadcasting for many years, comments:

I know that nothing, or almost nothing, arouses the fury of the British listening or viewing public as much as bad language in the inappropriate context or time. I did a programme about the contemporary artist, David Hockney, many years ago, in which he used the 'c' word when describing an etching by Picasso. He said, '*Look, he's looking at her c****' There wasn't a single complaint and two and a half million people watched that programme. Now, if you'd said that at seven o'clock, on that same evening, on that same channel, the lines would have been jammed. There's a certain sense in that because it's coming into a family context - this is a time when anybody from three upwards is listening and/or watching. So the family idea is taken quite seriously, or very seriously, by the British public.

Children are now far less protected from 'bad' language than they were even twenty years ago. Four letter words are written up all around them and used with energy and vitality by many of their favourite heroes. Many school-aged children are familiar with 'forbidden' expressions and have, at an early age, to know when they can get away with them. Swearing has become so commonplace, it has lost its potency.

FREEZING
THE RIVER

François Rabelais (1483 - 1553) is best known for his romance 'La vie de Gargantua et de Pantagruel' It is a chaotic 'history of giants' full of learning, coarse humour and flights of fancy. Rabelais delighted in a rich and picturesque vocabulary.

From the start of these journeys along the routes of English, we have followed the track of the spoken language as it winds across the landscape of our nation's history. We have seen it flow out of, as it were, the narrow gully of Anglo-Saxon Winchester and be shaped and channelled by the arrival of the Normans, who in turn forever changed its course.

Flowing onwards, this great river of English grew wide and strong as the flood of loan words engulfed and expanded it during the Renaissance. Now English is a mighty force, the tool of many of the world's greatest writers, the most powerful articulator and vehicle of expression in the world, greater than Latin for expressing ideas and new concepts in the sciences. By the twentieth century this river is like a linguistic Yangtse, so wide in its influence you can no longer make out its confines. It has ceased to be a great river; it has become a vast sea of language.

It was a French writer, François Rabelais, the great satirist and bawdy teller of tales of the Renaissance, who, in 1552, created the image of an ocean of words. His hero, Pantagruel, sailing with his companion Panurge on a journey across the high seas, encounters strange icebergs which, when heaved on deck, melt and let forth all sorts of sounds. These are frozen words, it transpires, which, in unfreezing, release the cries of a terrible winter battle that had occurred the year before. The words had been locked up within them ever since:

'Pantagruel then threw us on the deck whole handfuls of frozen words, which seemed to us like your rough sugar-plums, of many colours. And when we had somewhat warmed them between our hands, they melted like snow and we really heard them, but could not understand them, for it was a barbarous gibberish.   Panurge threw three or four handfuls of them on the deck; among which I perceived some very sharp words, and some bloody words, some terrible

words, and some others not very pleasant to the eye.

When they had been all melted together, we heard a strange noise, hin, hin, hin, hin, his, tick, tock, taack, bredelinbrededack, frr, frr, frr, bou, bou, bou, bou, bou, bou, bou, bou, track, track, trr, trr, trr, trrr, trrrrr, on, on, on, on, on, on, ououououon, gog, magog, and I do not know what other barbarous words, which the pilot said were the noise made by charging squadrons, the shock and neighing of horses...'

It is a fantasy dreamed up by a man for whom words were an eternal feast, born of an age of discovery and voyages into mysterious and uncharted waters where who-knows-what mysteries and wonders were to be found. Rabelais' notion of trapping the untrappable, of somehow fixing this great flow of language, which issues constantly from people's mouths, still catches the imagination five hundred years on. What if we *could* freeze the flow, stop the eternal shifting, evolving mass of English? What if, just for a moment, we could say 'this is now the state of the language'? However, just as we cannot stop time itself, or in reality freeze words, we cannot hold on to English and fix it even for an instant.

For each day brings a new context to describe, in different terms maybe, a new idea or

Dr. Samuel Johnson (clasping a walking stick in the forefront of the picture) was a writer and journalist and famous for his dictionary published in 1755. Here he is seen walking in Fleet Street with his friend, James Boswell who admired his work and wrote a biography of him.

fashion, a graphic event to be interpreted, news to be caught on the wing. Who would have thought, for example, a couple of years ago that the word 'zone' would, under London's Millennium Dome, take on a whole new life, a new emphasis? When cloning was first achieved, who would have thought that 'Dolly' would come to be a linguistic emblem of progress, or that you would be quite content to find a 'mouse' sitting next to your computer, or 'rocket' in your salad?

And these are merely things that are new to us or evolving new interpretations. What about the way we talk about these things. For years, stoical patients *fought* chronic diseases, and battled *against* incipient demise. Now most newspaper journalists and many broadcasters are content to describe brave sufferers as *battling* cancer.

However, it is still mainly Americans who *write* people or *protest* the war in the Balkans.

In Britain, we still prefer to write *to* our friends and protest *about* the refusal to import British beef.

It is very difficult to stop speakers from expressing themselves in these alternative (or as Americans would almost universally now say *alternate*) ways. Are they 'wrong' or merely different? Getting one's English 'right' is a real preoccupation in Britain. BBC listeners and viewers regularly bombard the broadcaster with complaints about instances of language 'misuse' on air.

When asked what grammatical errors drove them to distraction, Radio 4 listeners came back with the well-known and well-worn responses, like split-infinitives and the supposed misuse of the word 'hopefully'. Years of having grammar drilled into us as pupils at school has, it seems, resulted in a real wish to peg down 'correct' usages for ever.

Many of these critical radio listeners were no longer young and resented the newer terminologies and usages. They wished to 'make a stand' against the changing use of words like disinterested, infer, crescendo etc. One correspondent inveighed against the use in the first series of *The Routes of English* of the word *restauranteur* (with a redundant 'n'). It is, indeed, a solecism, and the dictionary confirms it. Yet the word may well be changing shape. It is now an English word, not just a French one in quote-marks, and, understandably and rightly, it begins to behave like an English word. And this process of assimilation, of language-change, has been the motor behind the development of English since it began.

Language-change is often seen as the result of an influence - and usually a negative one - from overseas. While embracing many aspects of American culture, many users of spoken British English resent what they see as the creeping Americanisation of British English. They object to the increasing use of such terms as *regular* to describe *standard* measures of things like coffee and soft drinks and the favouring of expressions such as *do you have?*, where they would have preferred *have you got?* It seems inevitable that with increasingly global communication directly into our homes via television, radio, cheap international telephone-calls and the Internet, it will be even more impossible than ever to freeze the river. Language change seems to be accelerating. New terms are joining the language at a rate greater than ever in the history of English. New usages for old words are driving out traditional meanings. Who would consciously call any dashing young man a *gay boy* these days without adding an explanatory rider? So why even try to fix the language?

There is little doubt that the ideas of 'correctness' that **Dr. Lynda Mugglestone** of Pembroke College, Oxford has described in relation to issues of class (chapter 3) arose from a corresponding desire to 'fix' the language. She points to the call (in 1712) by Jonathan Swift to establish an Academy of English and to Addison's appeal in 'The Spectator' a year earlier for linguistic governance. In fact, there had then been for a couple of decades a ferment of interest in the state of English. As we said at the start of this chapter, it had expanded hugely during the Renaissance, but many thought it had become unruly, unrefined and barbarous. It needed taming, ordering.

There was then flood of studies, manuals and, above all, the first serious catalogues and dictionaries. As **Professor David Crystal**, author of the Cambridge Encyclopaedia of the English Language and consultant to *The Routes of English*, has written, Dr. Johnson's dictionary of 1755 was 'the first major effort to impose order on the language'. Richard Mulcaster, Headmaster of Merchant Taylor's school in London in the late sixteenth century and an often-quoted source of linguistic observations, had in 1582 uttered a fervent wish that a dictionary be established containing 'all the words we use'. But apart from catalogues of 'hard words', only one person, Nathaniel Bailey, in his 'Universal Etymological Dictionary' of 1721, had sat down to make a comprehensive list of the English lexicon. Until Samuel Johnson set out on his great task.

Johnson, the opinionated and overweening intellect that we see refracted through James Boswell's 'Life', was a prodigious figure. Boswell, his companion and chronicler for more than twenty years described his mentor as:

'...correct, nay stern in his taste; hard to please, and easily offended; impetuous and irritable in his temper, but of a most humane and benevolent heart; having a mind stored with a vast and various collection of learning and knowledge, which he communicated with peculiar perspicuity and force, in rich and and choice expression. He united a most logical head with a most* *fertile imagination...'*

Samuel Johnson's 'Dictionary of the English Language' was published in 1755, the fruit of seven years' work largely completed at his house in Gough Square in London. 40,000 headwords are given definitions illustrated from writers of quality since Elizabethan times (though not from his own age). In Boswell's view, the Dictionary 'conferred stability' on the English language. Lynda Mugglestone and David Crystal, on the other hand, are both at pains to point out that Johnson's intention in the dictionary itself (as opposed to the plan for it that he published in 1747) was not to *pre*scribe, but to *de*scribe the language he found. Curiously, one might conclude that he had less in common with today's would-be Canutes, who write protesting at 'declining' standards of English, than is sometimes claimed.

However, the latter half of the eighteenth century was a period in which the idea of 'correct English' gained a prominence hitherto unheard of. Two hundred or more works on grammar, rhetoric and other aspects of the structure and workings of the language were published and the first skirmishes took place in the battle of opinions about the prescriptive and descriptive approaches to language use. Manuals in correct pronunciation began to appear, notably the 'Pronouncing Dictionary of English' compiled by John (Elocution) Walker in 1774. Walker was passionate in his crusade for correctness.

The unruly and overgrown garden of an English language, enriched by the linguistic expansion occasioned by an ever widening world of science, ideas and possibility, was a problem to the tidy minds of the eighteenth century. Here was not Order. Art and architecture, music and literature might be enjoying the fullest flush of the classical

In Veritate et Caritate

sense of order and symmetry. Yet the language was still unkempt. Across the Channel, French had been shorn of many of what were seen as vulgarisms. The rich, wild and fantastic vocabulary of Rabelais' Gargantua and Pantagruel, with their frozen words and other far more earthy adventures, had been culled by the language censors of the court of the Sun King, Louis XIV. The vocabulary of seventeenth-century Versailles had been shrunk to a few thousand words with the excision of anything deemed barbarous or vulgar.

This culture of policing language is, of course, one which the French take seriously to this day, with the so-called 'Immortals' of the Académie Française (founded by Cardinal Richelieu in 1635) still offering formal prescriptive judgements about the French language. French grammar has, naturally, undergone many assaults similar to those of its English counterpart, yet even today many relatively unlettered Frenchmen and women can, usually with a wry smirk, indulge in a piece of linguistic archaism, amending someone's modern usage with the formal yet old-fashioned more "correct" form. Likewise, the Académie has in recent years proscribed the use of many hated Americanisms which it has seen as attacking and subverting the French linguistic and cultural heritage. Such victims over the past twenty years have ranged from such modern inventions as the *fax*, the *Walkman* personal stereo and computer *software*.(Say *la télécopie*, not le *fax* , le *balladeur*, literally '*stroller*', not le *Walkman* and le *logiciel*, not le *software*) to such professionals as film cameramen (say *le cadreur* - '*framer*' - not le *caméraman*).

The French tradition is interesting to students of English because, despite the strong

lobby for control and authoritative prescription, this country has always resisted the formal establishment of an Academy to legislate on matters of linguistic correctness. This seems to bubble up out of the British character as much as directly from issues of language. How could a nation that has produced such a genius of unfettered language creation and manipulation as Shakespeare submit to the controls of some central governing authority?

King Louise XIV of France (1638 - 1715), known as the Sun King because of the extravagance of his Court's taste and lifestyle. His lavish palace at Versailles was celebrated throughout Europe as a centre of culture where vulgarity of any sort was deplored and where manners and speech had to conform to the highest standards of decorum.

And yet, in the spirit of putting some order into that unruly garden of English, the end of the eighteenth century saw the establishment of the first formal rules of English grammar. Notable were the works of Robert Lowth, a Winchester born scholar and cleric, whose 'Short Introduction to English Grammar: with Critical Notes' was published in 1762, and of Lindley Murray. Murray was born in America, but retired to England and here published his 'English Grammar' in 1794.

Lowth's principle was to 'lay down rules and to illustrate them by examples'. This was prescriptive grammar at its most essential. And the notion that it ecapsulates - that there is a correct way (and many incorrect ways) to form the structures of English - is central to grammatical prescription to this day. Do say 'between you and me', don't say 'none of the above are true'. However, as we all know all too well, many very expensively educated people say both 'between you and I' and 'none are...'.

The fact is that *spoken* English frequently 'breaks the rules'. We don't speak in complete sentences (if we speak in sentences at all, that is), we constantly start sentences with a conjunction (like 'and' or 'but') and sprinkle our conversation with split infinitives and 'hopefullys'. Spoken English is difficult if not impossible to 'fix'. Freezing this river is an impossibility. And while many would wish it otherwise (note the conjunction at the start of *that* sentence!), strictly ungrammatical usages like 'different than' and 'the Government are' are going to crop up regularly. Simply because that's what people say. And, as we said at the beginning of this chapter, the river of language is unstoppable, unfreezable. What we can do effectively is to observe usage and describe it. It is this that most linguists today would claim to do. The correspondents to Radio 4 who vigorously deprecate the use of disinterested to mean 'lacking an interest in' and enormity to signify 'enormousness' are correct in that the words are often 'misused' (in respect of their dictionary definitions).   However, unlike the person caught speeding in a built-up area, it is not possible to prosecute or even reprimand someone for such a misuse.

It offends, because if you happen to know the distinction, say, between disinterested and uninterested, there is a sense of the language being debased, of a refinement of meaning being lost. But, as we have seen so often while following these routes of English, the language evolves, meanings change, verbs become nouns, nouns are forced into verbal structures as the river flows on.   While English is not subject to the sort of legislation that can outlaw a word like *le caméraman* in French, it will evolve unchecked. And it is that unfettered freedom to do what we damn well like with our words that is the glory of English, that enabled Shakespeare to enrich the language with new words - evocative ones like 'incarnadine', but also the humbler ones like 'lonely'.

Nineteenth-century Britain saw a host of dictionaries. Fixing the language, offering definitions and etymologies was a Victorian passion. It culminated with the work of James Murray whose 'New English Dictionary' was first conceived by the British Philological Society in 1857. Murray was appointed and started work twenty years later, but what started as a relatively circumscribed project became one of the greatest linguistic undertakings of all time, a task whose dimensions became analagous to the vast cathedral building projects of the Middle Ages. The final volume did not roll off the presses until 1928, seventy-one years after the idea was mooted. The 'Oxford English Dictionary' (OED), which is the name by which Murray's work came subsequently to be known, is still pre-eminent amongst books of reference on the English language. It is an international work of reference which in hard-copy text runs to twenty large volumes.

Now in its full second edition, with a third proposed, the OED has recently taken the decision to move to electronic publication via the Internet. This is seen as a way of

introducing a greater degree of flexibility into the editorial process. The task of freezing the river has grown increasingly difficult as the pace of twentieth century life has accelerated.

Other interesting attempts at catching the essence of contemporary usage of spoken English were undertaken during the early 1990s. The British National Corpus was a joint undertaking involving several British dictionary publishers and universities as well as many fieldworkers. The intention was to collect, via in some cases tape-recordings, examples of English being used in natural unconscious situations. This was the ultimate in descriptive word-study, as the purpose that lay behind the project, at least in part, was to collect unmediated language use caught out of the air, unscripted, unprepared, uncorrected.

Another project, largely drawn from a wide variety of printed sources and going well beyond the obvious newspapers and periodicals is The Bank of English, set up by the Collins-Birmingham University International Language Database (COBUILD). Again, descriptive in nature, the Bank of English offers further uncorrected source material, collated on an interactive computerised database, of several thousand terms in current usage. These recent endeavours, then, are purely descriptive. They do not at any stage attempt to go beyond the snapshot of the language to say 'thou shalt not...' And, as we have seen, attempts to prescribe the spoken English of Britain are today doomed to failure. People will do what they want, whether it is 'correct usage' to do so or not. Some may tut-tut, others may feel inwardly superior for knowing that a solecism has been committed, but it is above all usage that largely determines the shape of the language today.

When Johnson was compiling his dictionary and 'Elocution' Walker was describing the required pronunciation to avoid what he called the 'peculiarities' of regional dialects, few made extensive forays beyond their home parish. A journey to the capital, if undertaken at all, was the experience of a lifetime for most. People stayed put and spoke the way they always had spoken. Such a stable state made the very idea of prescription possible.

Compare today's physical and social mobility, the access to information and diverse opinions and forms of expression via radio, television and the Internet. Compare the rapid changes in language fashions - they barely last a matter of weeks nowadays before obsolescence sets in - and the need for some more responsive means of catching the reality of current usage is required. A publication like Oxford's 'Dictionary of New Words' from the early 1990s was an attempt to corral recent coinages, yet this rapid evolution of popular language means that, like any attempt to freeze the language, it can only ever be a partially satisfactory solution. OED's on-line lexicon may be able to offer greater flexibility and be more reactive to the shape of language as we embark on the 21st century. It will be more a sluice-gate or weir across the river, perhaps, than a handful of frozen words.

Despite all this laissez-faire descriptivism, there has always been an enormous desire amongst the British for a guide to how they should speak; a tool with which to judge linguistic 'line-calls', and the 1996 revised third edition of Fowler's 'Modern English Usage' has continued to sell extraordinarily well since publication.

Let us conclude this volume of *The Routes of English* with the words of the pre-eminent lexicographer of the late twentieth century, Dr. Robert Burchfield, who edited it and who previously had been General Editor of the 'Oxford English Dictionary'. In his Preface to the new 'Fowler', he takes an enlightened and profoundly realistic view of the state of English:

It is written at a time when there are many varieties of standard English, all making different choices from the material notionally available to them. It is also a time when pessimists are writing gloomily about declining standards, the loss of valuable distinctions in meaning, the introduction of unappetising vogue words and slang. But I refuse to be a pessimist. I am sure that the English language is not collapsing - more severe changes have come about in past centuries than any that have occurred in the twentieth century - and in the English language, used well, we still have, and will continue to have, a tool of extraordinary strength and flexibility.

Picture Credits

The Routes of English is presented by Melvyn Bragg

Editor:Simon Elmes
Producers: Simon Elmes and Tom Alban
Researcher: Emma-Louise Williams
CD producer: Neil George

Sincere thanks are due to the many experts who have shared their enthusiasm and wealth of knowledge with the Routes team throughout the series:
Dr. Kathryn Lowe, Glasgow University
Professor David Crystal
Professor Roy Porter, the Wellcome Institute
Helen Dunmore
Dr. Denis Smith
Jonathan Betts, Curator of Horology, the Royal Greenwich Observatory
Elizabeth Knowles, Oxford Unversity Press
SImon Luke
John Ayto
Professor Walter Redfern, Reading UniversitySteve Punt
Dr. Carol Fox
Professor Peter Holland, Birmingham University
Professor Richard Hoggart
Dr. Laura Wright, Cambridge University
Justin Champion, Royal Holloway College
Professor Geoffrey Hughes
Professor John Wells, University College, London University
Dr. Lynda Mugglestone, Oxford University

Deep gratitude to BBC colleagues on the series:
James Boyle, Controller Radio 4, for his unwavering backing of the project
Christine Saunders, Broadcast Assistant, for putting up with all of us.

Bibliography

Twentieth Century Words - a dictionary compiled by John Ayto
Oxford English Dictionary
Oxford Dictionary of New Words
Cambridge Encyclopaedia of the English Language compiled by David Crystal
Dictionary of the English Language 1755 Samuel Johnson
Pronouncing Dictionary of English 1774 John Walker
Critical Pronouncing Dictionary 1791 John Walker
New English Dictionary 1857 James Murray
Dictionary of New Words
Modern English Usage Henry Fowler
Universal Etymological Dictionary 1721 Nathaniel Bailey
Short Introduction to English Grammar: with Critical Notes 1762 Robert Lowth
English Grammar 1794 Lindley Murray
Routes of English Book1 Simon Elmes
Talking Proper: the Rise of Accent as Social Symbol 1997 OUP Lynda Mugglestone
Language Play David Crystal
The Uses of Literacy Richard Hoggart
Noblesse Oblige 1956 Nancy Mitford
Puns(1984)l Water Redfern
The Road to Wigan Pier George Orwell
The Arte of English Poesie 1589 George Puttenham
Course of Lectures Thomas Sheridan
Jokes and their Relation to the Unconscious Sigmund Freud
Shakespeare's Wordplay 1979 M.Mahood
Shakespeare's Bawdy 1947 E. Partridge
The Canterbury Tales Geoffrey Chaucer
Finnegan's Wake James Joyce
Alice in Wonderland and Alice Through the Looking Glass Lewis Carroll
Plays Shakespeare
The Pelican and other nonsense verse Edward Lear
A Few Late Chrysanthemums John Betjeman
Pygmalion Bernard Shaw
Sybil; Or, The Two Nations Benjamin Disraeli
Lady Chatterley's Lover DHLawrence
La Vie de Gargantua et de Pantagruel Francois Rabelais
A Social History of Foul Language, Oaths & Profanity in English, 1998, Geoffrey Hughes
Life of Samuel Johnson James Boswell